GUIDE TO
CONTEMPORARY
LITERATURE

Salman Rushdie

SERIES EDITORS
Jonathan Noakes
and
Margaret Reynolds

Also available in Vintage Living Texts

Martin Amis

Margaret Atwood

Louis de Bernières

Sebastian Faulks

Ian McEwan

Toni Morrison

Jeanette Winterson

VINTAGE
LIVING
TEXTS

Salman Rushdie

THE ESSENTIAL GUIDE
TO CONTEMPORARY
LITERATURE

Midnight's Children

Shame

The Satanic Verses

V

VINTAGE

Published by Vintage 2003

2 4 6 8 10 9 7 5 3 1

Copyright © Jonathan Noakes and Margaret Reynolds 2003

The right of Jonathan Noakes and Margaret Reynolds to be identified
as the authors of this work has been asserted by them in accordance with
the Copyright, Designs and Patents Act, 1988.

First published in Great Britain in 2003 by Vintage
Random House, 20 Vauxhall Bridge Road,
London SWIV 2SA

Random House Australia (Pty) Limited
20 Alfred Street, Milsons Point, Sydney,
New South Wales 2061, Australia

Random House New Zealand Limited
18 Poland Road, Glenfield,
Auckland 10, New Zealand

Random House (Pty) Limited
Endulini, 5A Jubilee Road, Parktown 2193, South Africa

The Random House Group Limited Reg. No. 954009
www.randomhouse.co.uk

A CIP catalogue record for this book is available from the British Library

ISBN 0 0994 3764 3

Papers used by Random House are natural, recyclable products made
from wood grown in sustainable forests; the manufacturing processes
conform to the environmental regulations of the country of origin.

Typeset by Palimpsest Book Production Limited, Polmont, Stirlingshire

Printed and bound in Great Britain by
Bookmarque Ltd, Croydon, Surrey

CONTENTS

VINTAGE LIVING TEXTS: PREFACE

SALMAN RUSHDIE

VINTAGE LIVING TEXTS

Midnight's Children

Shame

The Satanic Verses

VINTAGE LIVING TEXTS: REFERENCE

Acknowledgements

We owe grateful thanks to all at Random House. Most of all our debt is to Caroline Michel and her team at Vintage – especially Marcella Edwards – but also to Ali Reynolds, Jason Arthur and Liz Foley, who have given us generous and unfailing support. Thanks also to Philippa Brewster and Georgina Capel, Michael Meredith, Angela Leighton, Harriet Marland, Louisa Joyner, to all our colleagues, and to our partners and families. We would also like to thank the teachers and students at schools and colleges around the country who have taken part in our trialling process, and who have responded so readily and warmly to our requests for advice. And finally, our thanks to Salman Rushdie for his work without whom . . . without which . . .

VINTAGE LIVING TEXTS

Preface

About this series

Vintage Living Texts: The Essential Guide to Contemporary Literature is a new concept in reading guides. Our aim is to provide readers of all kinds with an intelligent and accessible introduction to key works, of contemporary literature. Each guide suggests techniques for reading important contemporary novels, and offers a variety of back-up materials that will give you ways into the text – without ever telling you what to think.

Content

All the books reproduce an extensive interview with the author, conducted exclusively for this series. This is not to say that we believe that the author's word is law. Of course it isn't. Once his or her book has gone out into the world he or she becomes simply yet another – if singularly competent – reader. This series recognises that an author's contribution may be valuable, and intriguing, but it puts the reader in control.

Every title in the series is author-focused and covers at

least three of their novels, along with relevant biographical, bibliographical, contextual and comparative material.

How to use this series

In the reading activities that make up the core of each book you will see that you are asked to do two things. One comes from the text; that is, we suggest what you should focus on, whether it's a theme, the language or the narrative method. The other concentrates on your own response. We want you to think about how you are reading and what skills you are bringing to bear in doing that reading. So this part is very much about you, the reader.

The point is that there are many ways of responding to a text. You could concentrate on the methods you might use to compare this text with others. In that case, look for the sections headed 'Compare'. Or you might want to do something more individual, and analyse how you are reacting to a text and what it means to you, in which case, pick out the approaches labelled 'Imagine' or 'Ask Yourself'.

Of course, it may well be that you are reading these texts for an examination. In that case you will have to go for the more traditional methods of literary criticism and look for the responses that tell you to 'Discuss' or 'Analyse'. Whichever level you (or your students) are at, you will find that there is something here for everyone. However, we're not suggesting that you stick solely to the approaches we offer, or that you tackle all of the exercises laid out here. Choose whatever most interests you, or whatever best suits your purposes.

Who are these books for?

Students will find that these guides are like a good teacher. They introduce the life and work of the author, set each novel in its context, explain key ideas and literary critical terms as they arise, suggest comparative exercises in a number of media, and ask focused questions to encourage a well-informed, analytical approach to reading the novels in a way that is rigorous, but still entertaining.

Teachers will find in this series a rich source of ideas for teaching contemporary novels and their contexts, particularly at AS, A and undergraduate levels. The exercises on each text have been tailored to meet the various assessment objectives laid down in the subject criteria for GCE AS and GCE A Level English Literature, and are explained in such a way that they can easily be selected and fitted into a lesson plan. Given the diversity of ways in which the awarding bodies have devised their specifications to meet these assessment objectives, a wide range of exercises is offered. We've had fun devising the plans, and we hope they'll be fun for you when you come to teach and learn with them.

And if you are neither a teacher nor a student of contemporary literature, but someone reading for your own pleasure? Well, if you've ever wanted someone to introduce you to a novelist's work in a way that will let you trust your own judgement and read more confidently, then this guide is also for you.

Whoever you are, we hope that you will enjoy using these books and that they will send you back to the novels to find new pleasures.

All page references for *Midnight's Children*, *Shame* and *The Satanic Verses* refer to the Vintage editions.

Salman Rushdie

Introduction

In the interview included here you will see that Salman Rushdie speaks movingly about the moment, during work on one of the many drafts of *Midnight's Children*, when he realised that he had found his own voice. It was as exciting when he told the story to us, as it must have been when it happened. And little wonder, because that voice – so distinctive, so wise, so shrill, so clever, so funny – is like no voice heard before or, though it has had many imitators, since. Rushdie's work is so particular, in terms of subject matter, themes, setting, storytelling devices and formal literary method, that no one but he can speak in his tongue. Or tongues. Rushdie writes in English, but his mother tongue is Urdu. It's not the most important fact about his work, but it is one of the keys that unlock not just one space, but a whole city of rooms.

In the course of our interview Rushdie said, 'Me – I'm a city boy'. He was making a point about a radical difference in character between his own work and that of the South American writer Gabriel García Márquez (to whom he is often compared). But in fact the statement stands on its own. Salman may be a city boy, but Rushdie is a city writer. Whole tribes live in his work and there they multiply and grow to people worlds.

This is true of the many characters and generations of characters that appear in *Midnight's Children*, in *Shame* and in *The Satanic Verses*. But it is also true of the literary method that Rushdie uses. Rushdie has said that the guiding principle behind *Midnight's Children* is 'excess', just as his essential view of the character of India is one of excess, or – as he puts it – 'too muchness'. That 'too much' frames all his work. Even a brief glance at one paragraph will throw up allusions to classical myth, to an Indian song tradition, to films, to symbols and signs – and that's before you even begin on the language, which is likely to draw on obscure English idioms, Urdu, Hindi, and any number of European languages.

As with the references, so with his typical writing technique. Rushdie loves every kind of figurative language, so metaphors and similes and comparative conceits jostle with puns and wordplay and game playing of all kinds. You will find that we cite many examples in the reading activities that follow. But you will also find that you will be able to pinpoint many more.

There is a restlessness in this method which exactly matches the range of Rushdie's literary subjects. There are two terms that are often mentioned in relation to Rushdie: 'translation' and 'metaphor', and they each mean the same thing, a 'carrying across', the first from the Latin, the second from the Greek. This goes for Rushdie's subjects, too, where there is always a sense of movement, a 'carrying across' of one idea from place to place. Migration, for instance, is one of his key themes, and that measures 'home' against the place of 'exile' or displacement of whatever kind, including voluntary displacement. Identity, closely bound up with 'migration', is a second key theme, but his way of considering and analysing identity means that Rushdie recognises that that is what you do to 'create' a sense of who you are. His characters are never stable, monumentally integrated and consistent. They change, as the world changes. So 'metamorphosis' of all kinds is another theme, acknowledging that process of change, whether in the world around us or in ourselves. Dualities pattern Rushdie's literary vision: love and death; religious belief and religious fanaticism; generosity and cruelty; the state and the individual; the imperatives of history and the waywardness of the personal life. It is almost as though he cannot have one idea without immediately considering its opposite. But then the great triumph of his work – both in terms of methods and themes – is that it never becomes monolithic, no matter how large it may be, but succeeds in reconciling, coaxing, juxtaposing differences, teasing out connections.

In the interview Rushdie reveals that the first line of *Midnight's Children* was – at one point – a line that now occurs on page 19, 'Most of what matters in our lives takes place in our absence'. It is a statement about duality: there is a here, and there is a there. But in *Midnight's Children* the narrative knows that that is what it is. The line goes on, 'but I seem to have found from somewhere the trick of filling in the gaps in my knowledge, so that everything is in my head, down to the last detail'. And this is the 'trick' of Rushdie's fiction – it all seems to be there, even when it is not.

Perhaps this is one reason why Rushdie's blend of fact and fiction works so well, and earns his work so many admirers. At the end of the interview Rushdie says, 'We tell ourselves lies. And it's one of the jobs of the supposed writer of lies to unpack those lies and tell the truth.' Reference to 'real' events in the 'real' world figures in almost all of Rushdie's work, but there is a particular section in *Shame* where the narrator (who is and is not Rushdie himself) breaks off to discuss, in angry terms, a little group of true cases of racial attack and hatred, and of family abuses (pp. 115–18). Many critics were taken aback by this insertion of 'fact' into fiction and could not place the motive, the narrative perspective or the moral content. But the point is that in order to perceive what is real, it is sometimes necessary to resort to the imaginary. By definition, we can only ever experience life through our own senses, through our skin. Perception will always be subjective. While that is so, it is absolutely necessary for each one of us, every day, and pretty much at every moment, to engage in an act of imaginative construction. Only in that way can we see anything from anyone else's point of view. This is why fiction is so important. It's also why it is very often not fiction, but 'real', in that the efforts of our imagination are the closest we can ever come to an approximation of someone else's truth. There is a certain strand of Rushdie criticism that labels his work 'feminist'. This is not quite right, but there is a grain of truth in it – or two grains. Firstly, he does like women. But secondly, there is a sense in which his work occupies that zone which theoretical criticism describes as 'the other'. This kind of theory recognises that many of our cultural and literary discourses are framed around an assumption that there is a 'centre' which is 'absolute' (and white, male, European, upper class, educated) against which all that is 'other' is defined (black, coloured, female, racially elsewhere, without privilege, uneducated), and which – because it is secondary – must always be subservient. Rushdie's work is a work of *'ecriture feminine'* (as opposed to 'feminist') because he champions the second order. Or rather – more than that – he simply, uncomplicatedly, puts it first without a political agenda, even though he knows that there is one – and in that way his work challenges conventional order.

A quotation from Rushdie's essay 'Imaginary Homelands' may help.

It may be argued that the past is a country from which we have all emigrated, that its loss is part of our common humanity. Which seems to me self-evidently true; but I suggest that the writer

who is out-of-country and even out-of-language
may experience this loss in an intensified form. It
is made more concrete for him by the physical
fact of discontinuity, of his present being in a different place from his past, of his being 'elsewhere'
. . . human beings do not perceive things whole; we
are not gods but wounded creatures, cracked lenses,
capable only of fractured perceptions. Partial beings,
in all the senses of that phrase. Meaning is a shaky
edifice we build out of scraps, dogmas, childhood
injuries, newspaper articles, chance remarks, old
films, small victories, people hated, people loved;
perhaps it is because our sense of what is the case is
constructed from such inadequate materials that we
defend it so fiercely, even to the death.

Even in this short passage all Rushdie's themes appear.
Migration, difference, duality, creation, metaphor, 'too muchness', integration and a 'carrying across'. There is, in the end,
as there was in the beginning, a generosity in Rushdie's view
that lets in many things, and that never tries to force any pattern. A generosity that lets struggles, problems and differences
be as they are. And yet, paradoxically, by letting all those dis-
parate elements in, in all their individuality, his work does also
achieve a kind of reconciliation. At the end of the interview
Rushdie says that love is, more and more, at the centre of his
books. Perhaps it always was.

Interview with Salman Rushdie

London: 8 July 2002

JN: What was the thing that set you out on your novel, *Midnight's Children*? Was it to do with character, was it to do with the initial setting of Kashmir, was it to do with the whole question of Indian independence?

SR: No, it was just about childhood really. Before I even knew what the story of the book was, I had this idea of wanting to write a novel arising out of my childhood in Bombay, but also a novel about childhood. So that was the first impulse. And then I had an earlier aborted novel, about something else entirely, in which there was a minor character – a rather *different* minor character – called Saleem Sinai who was born at the moment of independence, and everything else about him in this other aborted manuscript was completely uninteresting. But for some reason that idea stuck in my head. And at some point I understood that he would be a useful vehicle. And I suppose it's because I was trying to write about my generation, and to have somebody born at the exact moment of midnight when I was born eight weeks earlier, seemed helpful.

So those two little things went together, and then only really in the doing of it did I discover the larger scale of the novel and this idea of its connection to history – that revealed itself to me as I was properly devising and beginning to write the novel. I had this very – perhaps romantic – memory of a very happy childhood. It's rather odd because Saleem doesn't have a very happy childhood, but I remember growing up in that city, at that time, as a very magical thing, and that was the germ, and linking Saleem's birthday to that, gave me the book.

JN: What was magical about this childhood in Bombay? What were the things that you remember?

SR: Well, the circumstances of Saleem's life are not unlike mine, in that he more or less grows up in my house and in my little neighbourhood. There we were on this tiny little hilltop above the city – this little group of houses – and it was an idyllic world for children, because it was all very safe: you could run around, there was virtually no traffic, the only cars that came up there – because it was a dead end – were owned by people who lived there, or their visitors. So we could all run wild, and we all knew each other in all these different houses and so we had a sort of extended family. It wasn't a family of blood, but it was a family of friendship. So it was a great space to be a child in. But also, of course, looking back at it from an adult perspective, it was a very interestingly mixed-up group, in that we were of every possible denomination and the families came from every possible part of India, and then also there were European and American families, and so we grew up among Hindus, Parsees, Christians, Buddhists, Sikhs, Jains, etc., who were all just our friends – and also Swedes, English people, Americans, Germans, Lebanese, people from all over the world who came there on a more temporary basis. It seemed normal.

JN: At the beginning of *Midnight's Children* there's the story of the sheet – the sheet with a hole in it, and I was very intrigued with the idea of this as a method, the idea of the part as opposed to the whole, and you almost do it in two ways: very philosophically, but also with language because then you start talking about the 'partitioned' woman, the 'sectioned' woman, the 'collage' . . .

SR: Well, having found the image of the sheet with the hole, it began immediately to feel like a metaphor for the way in which the whole book was written, and it became helpful to me as a way of understanding how to write the book. To fall in love with something seen only in little bits and to make the composite figure in your own imagination, and then fall in love with it, seemed not unlike what I was trying to do. So all those deliberate uses of phrases, such as the ones you mention, were there to steer the reader in that direction.

JN: But you can't ever resist . . . Once you've got hold of a pun, you do tend to play it out and pile up more and more.

SR: The essential philosophy of *Midnight's Children* is excess. Never do anything unless you do it to excess. Because I was really trying to find, not just a language, but a kind of manner that felt right for the subject matter. One of the things I thought about India was that India is not neat and restrained and highly selected and so on. India is crowded and excessive and vulgar and overblown and far too much for anyone to take in at any given time. So you have to have a literature of that kind of excess, of too muchness. That was one of the things I was trying to do. How do you put this huge cornucopia into a book? How do you put this vast crowd into a book? It seemed to me there were two ways. There's the kind of Jane Austen way, which is just to take one tiny strand – one hair from the head, and examine that in beautiful detail, and imply the rest from your examination of that single strand.

And there's the other, which is the Dickensian, Rabelaisian way, which is to try and pour it all in. And I guess I went down that road. So yeah, it goes too far, *Midnight's Children*. Its strategy is to go too far.

JN: But then in that case, given that you've got this huge cast of thousands and all these teeming multitudes, how do you go about particularising an individual character?

SR: Well, that's why it took so long to write.

JN: How long did it take?

SR: It took five years or something. Five years and more because, as I say, some bits of it had come out of abandoned work before that. Also I was much younger and I was more or less teaching myself how to write as I wrote it, so it was also that. It was a kind of learning experience for me. By the time I finished it I felt I had a much clearer idea about what sort of writer I was than when I began it. And I've always thought of it like that. That it was the book in which I learned who I was as a writer, and how to write my sentences, and how to offer stories which were nobody else's, which I don't think I understood before I wrote it.

But your question about particularising. Well, what's interesting about the major characters in the book is that I sort of stole the structure of my family in a simplified way. It's much less ramified in a way than my real family. Really, in order to make them come to life, I had to make them unlike people in my family. So the answer to your question about particularising is that I found that I deliberately had to push them away from people I knew, and give them characteristics and ways of thinking which were *not* like the real people. And then I could write them; then I found out who they were.

My grandfather once told me – when I was still quite young – much later when he actually was in India, no longer in Kashmir, he had been called as doctor to the house of a woman who was in purdah and her normal lady doctor was not available for some reason and he had been asked to examine her through a hole in a sheet, which he told me as a comedy story – he said this is a completely bizarre thing to be asked to do if you're a doctor, to put a stethoscope through a hole in a sheet and feel somebody's heart. So even for him, it was an extraordinary oddity that he'd once been asked to do this, and he told it to me in that way. So it stuck in my mind and in the end I used that story and made it happen to the grandfather in the novel. And it's in that way that the book really came to life. By putting together completely invented things and half-remembered things and actual people . . .

JN: . . . Then of course you draw the reader in, because we know about the sheet and the sheet keeps reappearing, like when it's used as the costume for the ghost . . .

SR: . . . And then it becomes the sheet through which Jamila sings her songs, etc. One of the structural devices that the book uses is the device of leitmotiv. The sheet is the most obvious of those but there's the silver spittoon . . . there's three or four things that recur through the book and sometimes people ask me, 'What does it mean? What's the meaning of the perforated sheet or the silver spittoon?' And I would say, 'Well, what it means is the sum total of all the moments at which it happens.' Because that's the way in which leitmotiv works. You bring it back at moments and it's a way of connecting those moments. And then you look at those moments together and that's the meaning of the motif . . . so I guess the sheet is one of those, and the spittoon is another and there are probably several others which I forget. I had to look for all kinds of organising devices to make comprehensible a book on this scale, and that was one of them.

JN: One of those organising principles that comes into my mind – and I take it that this was very self-conscious – is that we have this individual, sometimes bizarre, strange story being told about personal lives, and yet what is going on – very much in the background, almost offstage – is conventional history . . . two world wars, Hiroshima, all the rest of it. Were you aware of using that as a structural device almost . . . politically?

SR: Well, that – in the end – was the form the book took. It got there by stages rather than being where I originally thought I was going. But at some point I understood that if you have as your central device the idea of somebody whose moment of birth is identical to that of the moment of birth of the country in which he lives, that you can't then avoid that connection. Having made that connection – so obviously – at the very outset of the book, then it has consequences for the book. That's why I describe him as being 'handcuffed to history' and why I thought that in some ways he is doubly twinned. On the one hand he had this alter ego with whom he was exchanged at birth – and that's a kind of twinning – and another thing is the country itself is like a twin in that they are growing up together, and it became necessary to tell their story in that very closely connected way. It's a comic idea that becomes a sad idea, because the comedy is that he believes himself to be responsible for history – and this is so obviously an absurdist idea, because he's not . . .

JN: . . . History goes on anyhow . . .

SR: . . . But he claims, and he goes through increasingly elaborate explanations to prove, that everything that happens in the world happened in some way because of him or is connected to things that happen in his family, and so on ... So that the India–Pakistan war of 1965 – its secret purpose is to erase his family from the face of the earth. Now we accept this – we don't accept it literally, I think, or only semi-literally – we accept it and we don't accept it. We don't have to take it with the degree of seriousness that he takes it. But the thing that happens in *Midnight's Children* is that at the end of the second part, when actually a lot of his family is destroyed, he is – so to speak – unhoused, literally, because his house blows up.

After that, the third book of the novel, or the third movement of the novel, is the movement in which he actually is flung into history. Suddenly he doesn't have the cocoon of the family and private life and personal life around him, and the idea of the connection to history stops being a fantasy – he's actually in the middle of it. And of course what we then discover is that he's very much *not* the master of history – he's very much its victim. And what happens to him from then on in Bangladesh, and in the Emergency and so on and so on, is a kind of tragic answer to his claim to be responsible for everything. Although he still clings to it, in fact, he claims that the purpose of the Emergency is to eradicate him and all the other magical children. So that was the design of the book. That eventually he has to be confronted with the reality for which he claims to be responsible and obviously that's a kind of tragic confrontation. So that was – yes – very much a part of the design of the book. There's a *time* in the time of the book ... and dates and times are everywhere, very, very specific dates. Things happen at exact times on exact days. And, of course, the joke is that sometimes he's wrong. That sometimes when he says, 'Mahatma Gandhi died', he actually gets the death at the wrong time, he gets it in the wrong sequence. And one of the reasons for that was that I found when I was working on the book that memory plays tricks. You think you remember your life really well and you discover that you don't. So I decided to write a book in which somebody is remembering his life, and he quite often remembers it wrong, but even when he remembers it wrong, the book will favour his memory over the real events.

JN: That reminds me of a phrase from the novel: 'Most of what matters in our lives takes place in our absence.'

SR: Yeah ... well, in the first draft of *Midnight's Children* that was the opening sentence. In the first draft that's how it began, and then I thought, no, too much like *Anna Karenina* [by Leo Tolstoy], and it sets up the wrong sort of book. I think one of the things that's very important in *Midnight's Children* is the idea of the contract with the reader. What kind of a story am I going to tell you? I thought that that opening suggested a kind of Tolstoyan story ...

JN: ... Too much control on the part of the narrator?

SR: Yes, and I felt, it's an important thought, but I don't want it as the first thought. The reason that the book began like that, and the reason why in the book there's so much that happens before Saleem is born, is to say, 'We do not come naked into the world.' We bring with us an enormous amount of baggage, so therefore, limitation. And that baggage is history, family history and a broader history too, and we're born into a context, and we're born as the child of our parents, and as the descendant of our family, and as the people who live in a certain house, and there's a lot of stuff which is just given – which is not just ours to make. And in order to understand 'us', you have to understand that other stuff. Hence that kind of Whitmanesque beginning about having to 'swallow multitudes' and so on. That's what I meant by 'Most of what matters in our lives takes place in our absence'.

But not only that. History is one thing. But another thing that I think is really important, in all my writing, is a thought that I had about character in the contemporary novel. That is to say, the ancient idea of character being destiny. You know, 'a man's character is his fate', ever since Heraclitus – that's the idea. And it seems to me that there is something about the modern world that makes that not true any more. That's to say, a bomb drops on your house – it doesn't ask you whether you led a good life ... That is to say that there are now all kinds of gigantic global phenomena, whether they are economic or military or whatever they might be, which actually determine the fates of individuals – all of us – in a way that is completely beyond our control, and we're not even in those rooms. 'Most of what matters in our lives takes place in our absence.' Somebody causes a run on the pound on the Stock Exchange in New York and your company collapses in London ... And that's just a small example. In total war, character is not destiny. Bombs are destiny, economics, all sorts of things are destiny, other than character, and I thought ... if we have reached a point in the history of the human race at which that is true then there are consequences here for literature. You can't write in that old way, because that's no longer the only truth. I mean, it still is some of the truth, because we all respond differently to these events and in that sense one person who loses his job may respond differently to another person and that has to do with his character etc.

JN: So it's actually in complete opposition to a George Eliot version of 'Our deeds determine us, as much as we determine our deeds'?

SR: Yes ... But, you see, that may well have been true for her ... I just think we live in a different age and that we have to think again about what it is that moves us and shapes us and what our relationship as individuals is to those external forces. To what extent are we greater than they are? And to what extent are we less than they are? And that means something that I think I've tried to look at in all my books. So that's the long answer to why that was the first sentence of the book. Actually, I'm very pleased that you unearthed it, because it is a very important sentence, but I just took it away from the beginning because I thought that was less ... less declaratory, less rubbing the reader's nose in it.

JN: You have said that *Midnight's Children* is very much a book about the role of the reader, and I was intrigued at the way the relationship gets set up between Saleem and Padma – who is a version of the reader.

SR: Yes, that's what she's there to do. I think that's what she is about. The first draft of *Midnight's Children* was not written retrospectively. It didn't have that whole Padma frame narration, it was written just straight from the beginning to the end. And so she appeared as a character, but only at the end when she gets to the pickle factory, and not until then. And the pickle factory didn't appear until the end when he got the factory ...

JN: ... Ah, well, now the chutney runs all the way through ...

SR: ... Now it's there all the way through, and the other thing that is unusual about the first version is that it wasn't written in the first person. It was a third-person narration. And it took me ages to do it, but it didn't work at all. I ended up after having worked on it for a couple of years – more than a couple of years, maybe three years – with this enormous manuscript, slightly longer than the finished book, that just didn't work ... and it was very depressing ...

JN: . . . I'm not surprised . . .

SR: . . . And I knew that there was a book in there somewhere. There was this huge amount of material that had come out in a very fertile way, so I knew it was alive, but I also knew there was some real problem with it. And so I arrived at this restructuring of it really as a way of solving that problem, and partly I felt that there was a real difficulty in the original version in asking the reader to wait so long for the birth of the main character. And Sterne's *Tristram Shandy* still has the gold medal in the literature of delay . . .

JN: But with a very fine homage to it in *Midnight's Children* . . .

SR: Well, this is maybe like the *silver* medal, in its strategies of delay. But once you're deciding to tell the story before . . . clearly *Tristram Shandy* springs to mind, especially if your process is comic rather than not comic. But in the end I thought, well, maybe if he tells the story of the part before he is born, then at least for the reader he'll be there in the voice of the book and in the kind of consciousness of the book, and it will be easier for people to actually wait for him to show up, because he'll be there in all the sentences anyway. And then I thought, well, who is he telling the story to? And at that point, essentially, Padma walked in and sat down . . .

JN: . . . And started to harangue him . . . or you . . .

SR: . . . And that was *great* because, as I say, she'd been this minor character at the end of the story and then suddenly I had him sitting there writing his story and she just came into the room and I thought, oh, fine, it's you . . . and the thing that is great about her is that she is so down to earth and won't take any nonsense and so on and every time he goes off on some of his more rarefied and literary flights of fancy, she just tells him to get on with it, and I hope that what she does is to tell him exactly what the reader is feeling at that moment ... 'Oh, for Pete's sake' ...

JN: ... And she makes mistakes too, like when, at one point, she thinks that it's not Mumtaz who is going to be his mother, she thinks it's Alia.

SR: Yes. She's trying to guess, exactly, to guess the future of the story, and of course makes mistakes and so on ... and she becomes, yes, a kind of avatar of the reader. But I think the thing that makes her work is that she becomes very likeable in her own right. So she was a real discovery of the book. In the sense that she'd been a small figure at the end and she just made herself into a central character and became very important to the book's conception. And then this kind of retrospective narration gave me all kinds of other possibilities.

JN: What about the chutney then? When did that turn up?

SR: Well, again, the pickle factory was always there ... And when he gets to the pickle factory, I had, even in the original version, used the pickles as a metaphor for preservation, so after all, what he had embarked on is a kind of metaphor of preservation so that connection was always there, but it became much more foregrounded.

JN: Against the corruption of the clocks?

SR: Yes ... exactly. It just became so much easier to put all that up front in the story, once the pickle factory was at the beginning and once the whole story was being told from the pickle factory, and became a kind of alternative pickling. I had lots of fun with it. It was discovering something that was supposed to be a small metaphorical image at the end but became a dominating metaphorical image for the whole book.

But really I wanted to say that the great thing about having made that effort to rewrite the book in the first person ... I've always remembered the day when I began to do that, and I've always remembered it as the day I became a writer. The first paragraph of the book is not that dissimilar to what I wrote on that day – it got a bit pushed and shaped – but essentially I sat down and thought ... you know, 'born in the city of Bombay ... once upon a time'. And the moment that started coming out of me I felt this incredible *excitement* and energy and I realised that I'd actually discovered something which was not just the voice of the book, but was also *my voice*. And it started flooding out, pouring out, this kind of incredible thing came out of me and I thought, oh gosh, this is what it is, this is being a writer, this is knowing how to write a book, and it was so *exciting* ... even now, thinking about it, it's exciting ... and the book just poured out. After that I thought, oh well, I'm never going to be able to shut him up, because, as I say, the original idea was that maybe he'd only first-person narrate the bit until he was born, and I was not certain whether he needed to go on doing it, but the moment that thing started I thought, well, you'd be an idiot to stop this ... and just ... hang on to his coat-tails and let him run. And that was thrilling.

JN: So ... another first-person narration then, *Shame* ... Did that start off in the first person?

SR: *Shame* was a much more worked-out book from the beginning. I felt I knew much more what I was doing, and I didn't really want a dominant central character any more. *Shame* is a novel without a dominant central character. It has a character that it calls the hero, who is quite clearly not the hero – he's not the hero of anything – and it has a group of characters, all of whom are the central character in some part of the book. I had in my mind the image of ... if you imagine a circle of characters, and every so often a character steps into the middle of the circle, and then the book is seen from that point of view and then that character steps back and another one steps into the centre and the book is seen from that point of view. It's like a kind of dance ... I thought of it like that, and in part I thought of it like that as an antidote to Saleem. I thought, *this* time, I'm in charge.

So although there is Omar Khayyam Shakil and so on, he's really not, he's described in the book as somebody who's not even the hero of his own life, and I think not only is that true of him, but I think that's true of lots of people. In a way, that's why he became interesting to me – somebody who's a bit-part player in his own life story.

JN: Which is what happens very much at the end when he's being interrogated and he arrives at that confession and says, 'I am a peripheral man'.

SR: Yes, well, having written about somebody for whom ... the defining image of Saleem is the fantasy of being at the centre, and I thought this time I'd write about somebody who thinks of himself as being on the edge. So he is a kind of opposite to Saleem.

JN: He's also – and it is a theme that runs through all your books – kind of chopped up ... even this idea of having three mothers. Maybe it goes back to what you were saying about this very mixed-up society where you were growing up in Bombay, where there's lots and lots of different inputs, and not *one* source of origin.

SR: Partly, I think also, I was brought up very much in a female environment. In my family there's always been a serious boy shortage.

One of the things some people have said about my novels is why is it that, given people have this idea of women in India being demure and recessive, the women in my novels are the opposite of that? And I have said, 'Well, those are the women I knew.' In my family, if you wanted to make yourself heard, you'd better have a loud voice and something to say. Otherwise, there was plenty of competition for the air waves.

So one of the things I wanted to do with him was to describe somebody brought up in a tribe of women, and part of it came out of that. The triple pregnancy – I really don't know where it came from, I think it just happened. I hadn't been particularly planning that they would share the child. I think it just happened as I was writing and it seemed like a good idea.

I actually do plan books quite carefully, and *Shame* I planned very carefully. But I always felt that you have to leave yourself the possibility of having a better idea. And you have to have the flexibility that this is something more interesting than what you first thought of, and to see what that means in terms of reshaping the whole. And equally you have to be ready to say, 'Well, that may seem like a good idea, but it's not necessary and so out it goes.' So you have to be able to do that too. It's what Hemingway called 'the shit detector', you have to have that. And it's true that the book you finish is never the book you begin. You discover things you thought were important turn out to be less important, things you thought were not important become more significant, and incidents that you thought would take twenty-five pages to describe end up taking two paragraphs, and vice versa. So you can't quite tell. And as to that beginning – I was very happy with it when I found it and that's why it's still there, but I hadn't quite realised it was going to happen until it happened.

JN: One of the words I wrote down was 'improvisation' ... Obviously, say, in a later novel like *The Ground Beneath her Feet* that becomes a key idea, but is that a fair way of describing your method?

SR: Well, you see, I often think about books musically. I often think about the structure of books symphonically ...

JN: ... Yes, you used the word 'leitmotiv' earlier, didn't you?

SR: Yes, I do think about symphonic form and not just symphonic form, but, to use the Indian metaphor, the form of the *raag* ... and the point about that is that it's like jazz. There is a lot of room for improvisation inside a melodic structure. So if you look at the written-down form of a *raag* it's incredibly simple, because the performer makes it up, but makes it up within very strict rules – start here, go here, finish there. But it's like jazz and one of the interesting things is that there've been a lot of close connections between jazz musicians and Indian *raag* players.

But that idea, the idea of the performer being the composer, and of creation as being also performance, is very different from Western music in which the composer writes it and the performer plays it. Sure, interprets it, but essentially plays the notes. That's not true in the Indian tradition. The performance *is* creation. And the creation is performance, therefore. And that's something to do with why my stuff comes out the way it does. There is a kind of – what in the West you might call – jazz element to it. And I've always liked that – the discovery of the riff. There's a fair amount of riffs here and there in my books ...

JN: . . . Digressions, even . . .

SR: . . . Yeah . . . well, just that you get hold of something and you want to see where it goes, and you see it through and then you go back to 'as I was saying' . . . It seems to me that's quite like how people talk. If you look at the way people actually talk to each other and how they tell each other stories, that's how they do it, and it's only in literature that you're supposed to clean up that act, but I didn't see any reason to clean it up.

It's interesting, in *Shame*, one of the things that I remember when it came out that caused some consternation was the use of this kind of so-called non-fictional stuff set against the fictional . . . I mean, the bits where the author talks directly, or seems to talk directly to the audience, and then goes back into the fiction. And a lot of people thought, well, what's that about? You're not supposed to do that. Why is he doing that? And I thought, well, if I were telling you a story about anything, it would be quite natural for me to editorialise, and to say, well, what this reminds me of is so-and-so . . . or . . . something like this once happened to me, etc. And it seemed odd to me that something that is so natural in the spoken form seemed so problematic when written down. I didn't think I was doing anything particularly odd there, but a lot of people who read the book found that like a jolt. And I suppose, to an extent, it was supposed to be.

JN: I guess that it's similar to the Padma technique . . . letting the reader in there.

SR: Yes, except, no Padma. It's more direct, you get rid of Padma in favour of a direct address. It's a kind of trick, because the so-called ostensible author who is making the comments isn't really me. So it's an alternative fiction. It's a fiction pretending not to be a fiction and being set against a fiction that is self-evidently a fiction. So it's really not contrasting fiction with non-fiction, it's actually contrasting two different kinds of fictional process. That's why it seems odd. But of course it's supposed to make you stop and think. Books should make you stop and think.

JN: Well, yes! This improvisation though, letting yourself go in any direction. Does that make problems? Do you know when you've got to the end? Does that mean that it's difficult to *end* a book?

SR: No. One of the things I need to know before I start is where it's going. It doesn't always go there. But I need to have the feeling that I know where I'm getting to. And it usually does go there in terms of theme and mood and so on, but often what happens is the specific ending changes – because you discover it's not as great as you thought and you have to find something else. Sometimes it doesn't – for instance, in *Haroun and the Sea of Stories* originally I didn't think it would have a happy ending. I didn't actually believe that the nuclear family would be recreated at the end. I thought it would be a rather contemporary book in which ... you know, the little boy has to get used to the fact that he has a new relationship with his parents who are separated but it's all fine ... And then I thought, no: can't do it. The book is demanding a certain kind of reunion that you can't deny, and so in the end I had to allow the logic of the book to dictate.

JN: ... Did you know how *Shame* was going to end?

SR: ... Well, I knew it was going to end pretty violently. If you – at the beginning of the novel – create such a device as this ... what's called the dumb waiter, full of weapons ... then you know that at some point in the novel those knives are going to be unleashed. You can't just put them there for *nothing* . . . You've got to use them. So I did know that.

But with *The Satanic Verses* I didn't know. In *The Satanic Verses* the original last chapter was also about Saladin Chamcha going back to Bombay because his father was dying, but in the original version, by the time he got there, his father had already died. And that confrontation – reunion scene could never take place, and so he was essentially left with a lot of unfinished business and it was kind of painful. Though in a way that worked too.

JN: It's explaining the ways of God to man, in a sense, in terms of the relation between the father and the son, the creator and the created . . .

SR: Yes. But that was an ending I hadn't expected.

JN: You've mentioned several writers: Dickens, George Eliot, Sterne. One of the things that you do a lot is use other texts. You've also mentioned the 'once upon a time' that appears in *Midnight's Children* and it's in *The Satanic Verses* and *Shame* as well. How much of this – using other texts – is a game for you, or is it a serious preoccupation?

SR: It's just a way of getting going really. And sometimes it's – well, I suppose it's wrong to call it just a crutch because it's more than that – but . . . I don't know . . . books come out of other books as well as out of life. And I don't see any reason to disguise it. Nothing comes from nowhere. And with these books sometimes I've felt the need to *show* the literary ancestry because there's such a dominance *still*, in English literature particularly, of . . . you were saying George Eliot . . . of the kind of naturalistic tradition of the social psychological novel that I wanted to say, 'But there are other traditions.'

And the alternative great tradition of the novel is what Kundera called 'the children of Tristram Shandy'.

One of the things about growing up as I did is that you grow up surrounded by stories that are obviously not true. But by acknowledging openly their untruthfulness, they tell you truth, and that's why they're loved. They're not loved because they are not true – they are loved because they *are* true.

So if you go to India and Pakistan and ask about *Midnight's Children* and *Shame*, they're not talked about as fairy tales. In the West, people tended to stress their fantastical elements. In India that's not what happened. In Pakistan *Shame* was seen ... after all, the book does take as its starting place a real-life confrontation between a military dictator and a civilian politician, one of whom was elevated by the other and then became his executioner. I thought this was a kind of Shakespearean gift for a writer – for that to be a given, the idea that your protégé becomes your killer, and so I took it. And of course people in Pakistan understood where it was coming from and they saw it as an interesting portrait of what really happened, even though of course the book is in many ways very heightened and non-naturalistic.

JN: It's the difference almost between realism and naturalism?

SR: Yes. Naturalism is something mimetic and photographic. But I think all these novels are *extremely* naturalistic: the London of *The Satanic Verses* ... the Pakistan, the version of the Pakistan depicted in *Shame* ... the places and settings and people of *Midnight's Children* ... there's nothing fantastic about them. Growing out of them, there are some sorts of more exotic flowers. One of the writers that I learned this from was Dickens, because it seems to me that one of the things that is most interesting about Dickens is the fact that he manages to pull off the trick of having an incredibly meticulously naturalistically observed background, and to project against that a completely surrealistic foreground. So, for instance, the dust heaps of *Our Mutual Friend* express the idea of a civilisation being overwhelmed by its own garbage, but in that garbage there are treasures if you know how to look for them. That's not a naturalistic image. That's expressionism . . .

JN: . . . Except that – as you say – it is *real* because the perspective and the analysis and the moral make it real.

SR: The Circumlocution Office [in Charles Dickens's *Little Dorrit*] isn't real. And yet a government department that exists in order to do nothing *strikes* us all as real. That's the genius of Dickens.

And that was the lesson I tried to learn. If you're going to use fantastical elements, make sure that they are there in order to intensify our knowledge of the real world and not to escape it.

JN: I just want to ask you a couple of things coming out of *The Satanic Verses*, but actually they apply to all of your books, to do with particular kinds of themes that keep coming back. One is that you are very interested in what I can only call star quality – the charismatic personality that draws people to them is a recurring character. And the other is the question about love – that you are only recognised if somebody else believes in you, somebody else creates you . . . Those two themes – are they things that you recognise?

SR: Yes . . . and I think more and more. To an extent those preoccupations are there even in *Shame* – the very charismatic politician and the less charismatic general may have something to do with the former's murder by the latter.

JN: It's also there in *The Satanic Verses* because of the film-star world.

SR: Yes ... the film stars and the prophets and so on. It's become such a dominant thing in our age. The subject of the STAAAR – the person who we nominate for exceptionality, and then gleefully tear down if possible. It's a blood sport. And it's a religion, or a quasi-religion, and I've got more and more interested in it. I suppose *The Ground Beneath her Feet* is the one that deals with it most centrally, but yes ... There's a line in *Les Enfants du Paradis* [directed by Marcel Carné, 1945] where the Jean-Louis Barrault character says to the Arletty character, '*Les acteurs ne sont pas les gens*', 'Actors aren't people'. And I actually used that line somewhere in *The Satanic Verses*. So here are these two actors in *The Satanic Verses*, one of whom was ultra-visible and the other one was invisible. One is the most famous face in the country, and the other is the most famous voice. So they were in a way opposite kinds of actor – the visible and the invisible.

The book is about a conflict between the visible and the invisible worlds. The largest section of the novel is called 'A City Visible but Unseen' and it's trying to suggest that even among us there are massive millions of invisible realities. A thing that happens in India: you grow up in India and, as people tell you all the time, you stop seeing the poverty. You just physically stop seeing it because it's unbearable to see it. You actually can't lead your affluent life – the you I'm suggesting who owns a car and so on – you literally drive past and you don't see it. You blind yourself. And I've known it happen when people first come to India and are driven around and are shocked to see what there is, their friend, their Indian friend who's driving them around says, 'What do you mean? What are you talking about? Where?'

The level of celebrity is one thing. But what is seen and

what is not seen, but is nonetheless *there*, is something that is there in all my books.

JN: So is that partly why this question about being loved and being recognised – to be *really seen* – becomes so important?

SR: The subject of love gets closer and closer to the central concerns of my books as they go on. I do think exactly that. That love is about being seen. And seeing. And the other thing that I have increasingly is that it's not nearly as eternal. There are two ideas: one is duration, and the other is love. It seems to me what happens is that we put them together, and I don't think they necessarily have anything to do with each other. Yet we can't believe in love unless we also believe in its duration. One of the harsher truths that my books have grappled with is to try and separate those things. To try and say that they may not be related.

JN: Well, maybe the intensity that goes with one is not compatible with the other.

SR: One of the great things about love is that it never stays the same. In any loving relationship, it's never stable – it either gets better or it gets worse. Or it gets better and *then* it gets worse. Or it gets worse and then it gets better and then it gets worse again. But it changes all the time. Anybody who's ever been in a loving relationship knows that. And yet we have a myth of stability about it. We have a myth that you fall in love and that's it. But actually what we all know in our lived experiences is that that is *not it*. I've tried to write about that – how that's not it. On the one hand it's what we desperately need in order to feel recognised and known, and therefore we have to cling to the idea that once we've got it, we've got it. But actually it's very shifting soil. And that makes it scarier, but not less desirable.

We tell ourselves lies. And it's one of the jobs of the supposed writer of lies to unpack those lies and tell the truth.

Midnight's Children

IN CLOSE-UP

Reading guides for

MIDNIGHT'S CHILDREN

BEFORE YOU BEGIN TO READ . . .
— Read the interview with Rushdie. You will see there that he identifies a number of themes:

- Childhood
- Multiplicity
- Difference and integration
- Time
- Memory and mistaken memory
- The idea of history
- The contract with the reader
- First-person narration

Other themes that it may be useful to consider while reading the novel include:

- Absence and presence
- Storytelling
- Parents and children
- The author as reader

While you are reading *Midnight's Children*, *Shame* and *The Satanic Verses* in detail it is worth bearing the overall themes listed at the beginning of each reading guide in mind. At the end of each reading guide you will find suggested contexts, which will help you to situate the novel's themes in a wider framework. The reading activities given below are designed to be used imaginatively. Choose whichever sections most interest you or are most useful for your own purposes. The questions that are set at intervals are to help you relate parts of the novel to the whole.

Reading activities: detailed analysis

CONTENTS

Look at the Contents pages. Which headings suggest a focus on the mundane, and which suggest the exotic or the fabulous? Which headings suggest an eye for detail, and which suggest a grandly sweeping view? Which position something, in a place or in time, and which suggest the passing of time? What can you tell about the novel and its themes from these headings?

BOOK ONE

THE PERFORATED SHEET
SECTION 1 (pp. 9–10)

Focus on: openings and narrative voice

INFER . . .
— This is a first-person narrative: the narrator is a character in his own story. The narrator's 'voice' – his tone, his choice of words, his way of telling his story – are an integral part of his characterisation; so *how* the narrator speaks should be 'read'

as attentively as what he says. What impressions do you form of the speaker, Saleem Sinai, in this opening section?

Focus on: context

RESEARCH . . .

Rushdie talks in the interview about the central conceit that Saleem's personal history is 'handcuffed' to India's history (p. 9). His birth occurred at the symbolic moment when India was 'born' as a free nation – when she gained her independence from Great Britain – at midnight on 15 August 1947. The Prime Minister of independent India, Pandit Jawaharlal Nehru, announced that, 'At the stroke of the midnight hour, while the world sleeps, India will awake to life and freedom.'

— Research the events that led up to this moment: you might start by looking at this and associated websites: http://www.kamat.com/kalranga/freedom/index.htm

THE PERFORATED SHEET
SECTIONS 2–3 (pp. 10–23)

Focus on: imagery

TRACE AND ANALYSE . . .

— Look for images here that connect back with images in the opening section, or which form connections within this section, such as the three drops of blood, diamonds and rubies, rebirth, mutilation, a hole at the centre. What effects are created by these connections?

Focus on: the theme of telling stories

ASSESS . . .

— How does Rushdie draw the reader's attention to the idea

of 'telling stories' in this section? Consider Saleem's own comments on his love of stories, his narrative technique and the references to stories told by other characters.

DISCUSS . . .
— Consider and discuss the claim that 'Most of what matters in our lives takes place in our absence' (p. 19). It may be useful to refer back to the interview where Rushdie discusses this idea on pp. 17–19.

Focus on: the fantastic and the actual

TRACE AND EXAMINE . . .
— Rushdie often mixes the fantastic and the actual. Trace how this section combines the two in its account of events and of characters, and examine the effects created by this combination.

Focus on: Kashmir

RESEARCH . . .
— This part of the novel is set in Kashmir, in northern India. Research Kashmir, its culture and its history (especially during the twentieth century). You might start by using the website at http://www.jammukashmirinfo.com/Kashmir/

MERCUROCROME
SECTIONS 1–3 (pp. 24–30)

Focus on: narrative technique

ANALYSE . . .
— Consider and analyse the effects created by the interleaving of the narrative threads.

Focus on: points of view and gender

RETELL . . .

— In no more than 300 words, retell the story of Aziz's 'courtship' of Naseem from her point of view — and in her voice.

MERCUROCROME
SECTIONS 4–9 (pp. 30–7)

Focus on: the theme of innocence and experience

CONSIDER . . .

— Look at the various ways in which the theme of innocence and experience is developed in these sections. How are comic effects created, and how are serious effects created?

Focus on: cinematic techniques

ASSESS . . .

— Saleem comments that 'nobody from Bombay should be without a basic film vocabulary' (p. 33), a reference to Bombay's huge film industry. Assess how cinematic techniques are used in his narrative.

Focus on: context

CONSIDER THE EFFECT OF HISTORICAL ALLUSIONS . . .
References are made to Hartal (strike) Day (p. 33), a day of silence in protest against the British presence in India; to the Rowlatt Act (p. 33), which the British administration issued to secure 'emergency' powers for itself to prevent hartals; to Dyer's Martial Law regulations (p. 35); and to the massacre at Amritsar on 13 April 1919, when British troops under Dyer

opened fire on a peaceful demonstration against the Rowlatt
Act in a crowded plaza, killing an estimated 379 and wounding
at least three times that number. Nowadays the site, Jallianwala
Bagh, is a national shrine, and the massacre, which exposed
the moral injustice of British rule, is seen as marking a crucial
moment in the decline of the power of the Raj.
— What is the effect of alluding to real historical events in a
fictional narrative? And what significance do these allusions
have, coming at this stage in Saleem's narrative?

HIT-THE-SPITTOON
SECTION I (pp. 37–44)

Focus on: connections

TRACE AND COMMENT . . .
— The narrative playfully connects dissimilar things: Saleem's
body and the body of the Indian nation; cooking and writing;
writing and sex; domestic rules and sex; spit and sex and blood
and violence. Trace how these comparisons are made, and comment on the effects created by them.

Focus on: language

ANALYSE THE LANGUAGE . . .
— Read carefully the description of Naseem on pp. 40–3 ('She
had become a prematurely old . . . ". . . and kiss his, whatsitsname, feet!"'). Pick out the words and phrases which, in your
opinion, characterise her most effectively, and analyse the
effects created by these words.

HIT-THE-SPITTOON
SECTIONS 2–4 (pp. 44–51)

Focus on: the power of stories

CONSIDER AND DISCUSS . . .

✱ — 'Sometimes legends make reality, and become more useful than the facts' (p. 47). What is a 'legend'? Refer to the glossary of literary terms if you are unsure. What does he mean by a legend being 'more useful' than facts, do you think? How might this idea throw light on his narrative? Discuss the ways in which Saleem gives Hummingbird's story legendary qualities in these sections.

UNDER THE CARPET
SECTIONS 1–3 (pp. 51–9)

Focus on: noses and sense of smell

CONSIDER NOSES IN LITERATURE . . .

— Noses figure prominently in *Midnight's Children*. What significance does Saleem attach to them? Consider what significance noses have in other stories, such as Edmond Rostand's *Cyrano de Bergerac* (1897), Carlo Collodi's *Pinocchio* (1883), or Edward Lear's nonsense poem, 'The Dong with a Luminous Nose'. You might also like to look at *The Nose Book*, edited by Victoria De Rijke, Lene Østermark-Johansen and Helen Thomas (Middlesex University Press, London, 2001).

EXAMINE THE METAPHORS FOR SMELL . . .

— Draw up a list of as many expressions as you can think of that use metaphors for smell ('the sweet smell of success', for instance, or 'it gets up my nose' or 'to smell a rat'). How many metaphors does Saleem make out of the sense of smell in this section? Underline or list them. Examine what to 'smell' means in each case.

Focus on: realism and exaggeration

ASSESS . . .
— Assess the validity of the claim that the comic exaggerations of these sections depend for their success on being rooted firmly in realistic detail.

UNDER THE CARPET
SECTIONS 4–5 (pp. 59–64)

Focus on: comedy and tragedy

EVALUATE . . .
— Is Mumtaz's story comic or tragic? What effect is created by the reminder on p. 61 that on the same day (9 August 1945) an atomic bomb was dropped on the Japanese city of Nagasaki?

A PUBLIC ANNOUNCEMENT
SECTIONS 1–3 (pp. 64–73)

Focus on: the parts and the whole

ANALYSE THE NARRATIVE STRUCTURE . . .
Earlier Saleem has said: 'I seem to have found from somewhere the trick of filling in the gaps in my knowledge, so that everything is in my head, down to the last detail' (p. 19). This idea of the details that make up the whole occurs throughout: in the way Amina divides Ahmed 'into every single one of his

component parts, physical as well as behavioural, compartmentalizing him' (p. 68), for instance, or the way Aziz pieces together Naseem from glimpses through the perforated sheet. — See Rushdie's comments on this idea in the interview on pp. 11–14. Analyse the eclectic way the narrative is constructed in *Midnight's Children*, referring to these sections or more widely.

A PUBLIC ANNOUNCEMENT
SECTIONS 4–7 (pp. 73–8)

Focus on: racial and religious layers

LOOK FOR AND CONSIDER . . .
— List all the racial and religious groups and the way that they perceive each other. Consider the idea that, no matter how different groups of people may be, prejudice always wears the same face.

MANY-HEADED MONSTERS
SECTION 1 (pp. 78–80)

Focus on: storytelling

INTERPRET THE METAPHOR . . .
— You might have noticed several references already to the 'Anglepoised pool of light' which is mentioned again on p. 79. How does this image serve as a metaphor for the narrative vision?

MANY-HEADED MONSTERS
SECTION 2 (pp. 80–9)

Focus on: narrative technique

EVALUATE THE EFFECTS . . .
— Look over this section, which tells the story of Ahmed and Amina's visit to the Red Fort. What linguistic strategies does the narrator use to create a sense of events unfolding in the immediate present, and of multiple points of view?

MANY-HEADED MONSTERS
SECTION 3 (pp. 89–91)

Focus on: narrative delay

CONSIDER AND DISCUSS . . .
— Much to Padma's irritation, Saleem is still delaying his own entrance. Consider the significance of origins and antecedents in a sense of identity, then look at what Rushdie says about this connection in the interview on pp. 10–14. Why does Saleem delay his own entry for most of Book One? The chapter 'Tick, tock' will throw more light on the answer to this question.

METHWOLD
SECTIONS 1–8 (pp. 92–106)

Focus on: characterisation

ANALYSE . . .
— What is a 'stereotype' character, and why do novelists some-times use them? To what extent is Methwold a stereotype of

the colonial expatriate? What impressions do you form of him and of the language that he uses?

TICK, TOCK
SECTIONS 1–5 (pp. 106–20)

Focus on: time

ASSESS THE EFFECTS . . .

— Work through the chapter, noting all the references to time. Which look backwards, and which forwards? How does Saleem use the countdown to create a double sense of one world drawing to a close, and of another world arriving? Go on to consider how this two-way vision is central to the novel, including its title, *Midnight's Children*.

Focus on: dreams and the irrational

INTERPRET . . .

— Consider the elements of the story that suggest the prevalence of the irrational in Indian culture (superstitions, prophesies, astrology, curses, stories). 'It can happen. Especially in a country which is itself a sort of dream' (p. 118). What do you think Saleem means by this description of India as 'a sort of dream', and how has this characteristic been emphasised so far in the novel?

Focus on: identity and symbol

RESEARCH AND COMPARE . . .

— Read carefully the account of the birth of the two boys on pp. 117–18. The boy born at the same time as Saleem is 'Shiva of the knees'. In Hindu mythology, Shiva is the god of violence and destruction. Saleem, on the other hand, with his large ears and long nose, can be seen as representing Ganesha, the gentle god of literature and wisdom. Research Ganesha, and compare his nature with that of Saleem. What do these associations add to the story of the confusion of the two boys? And what does this story add to the theme of identity in Book One?

Looking over Book One

QUESTIONS FOR DISCUSSION OR ESSAYS

1. What are your impressions of Aadam Aziz? Consider which aspects of his character and of his heritage Saleem has sought to emphasise.

2. Discuss the notions of identity and belonging, as they are presented in Book One.

3. What impressions have you formed of Kashmiri social mores in the early twentieth century? Consider the significance of professional roles, of gender roles, of age and of status in your answer.

4. Compare and contrast the Sinai–Padma relationship with that of Aziz and Naseem. How influential are the contrasting social expectations of their different times on their relationships?

5. For whom is Saleem telling his story? Himself? Padma? The reader? What difference does it make?

6. Discuss the portrayal of marriage in Book One.

7. 'In a kind of collective failure of imagination, we learned that we simply could not think our way out of our pasts ...' (p. 118). Discuss the importance of 'the past' in Book One.

✱ 8. 'What's real and what's true aren't necessarily the same' (p. 79). Discuss, with reference to this narrative.

9. Discuss the ways in which Padma's commentary provides a moral perspective on the story being told.

10. Saleem is 'Midnight's child' (p. 119). Comment on the significance of time in Book One.

11. In what senses is Saleem represented as a symbol of the whole of India in Book One?

12. Explore the idea of 'the whole in parts' in Book One.

BOOK TWO

THE FISHERMAN'S POINTING FINGER
SECTION 1 (pp. 121–3)

Focus on: the relation between reader and text

COMMENT ON . . .
— Saleem asks if it is possible to be 'jealous' of written words (p. 121). Look carefully at section 1 of this chapter (pp. 121–3) and comment on Padma's relation a) to Saleem, and b) to Saleem's story. In what sense is Saleem in love with his own story? What is it that makes his story seductive?

RESEARCH AND COMPARE . . .
— Scheherazade has been mentioned several times since p. 24. If you do not already know *The Arabian Nights* find out about it, or read a version of it. What is the connection between sex and storytelling in Scheherazade's story? How might this be

compared with Saleem, his storytelling and his relation to Padma?

THE FISHERMAN'S POINTING FINGER
SECTIONS 2–4 (pp. 123–31)

Focus on: appetite

LIST AND ASSESS . . .
— As soon as he is born Saleem starts ingesting the world. Note down every time that the mouth, eating, swallowing and digesting are mentioned. How does this image of Saleem 'swallowing' everything connect to the metaphor of him taking in the life of a nation and of an historical time in the novel as a whole? You might look back to p. 9: 'I have been a swallower of lives; and to know me, just the one of me, you'll have to swallow the lot as well.' Think of the opposite functions of excretion, spitting out, vomiting and creating waste. How might these work as a metaphor for the narrative patterning of the novel as a whole?

THE FISHERMAN'S POINTING FINGER
SECTIONS 5–6 (pp. 131–6)

Focus on: puns

CONNECT . . .
— Spirits in a bottle, frozen assets . . . look at how Saleem develops these puns. How do they relate to his love of bizarre connections and patternings?

SNAKES AND LADDERS
SECTIONS 1–5 (pp. 136–49)

Focus on: omens

CONSIDER THE NARRATIVE FUNCTION . . .
— What is an omen? Look up the detailed meaning in a dictionary, preferably the *Oxford English Dictionary*. What other words are there for omens? Look for these in a thesaurus. How many omens does Saleem list in this chapter? How are omens and predictions for the future employed in terms of the narrative structure of *Midnight's Children* as a whole?

Focus on: metaphors

NOTE ASSOCIATIONS . . .
— What do 'snakes' mean metaphorically? What do 'ladders' mean? Look both up in a dictionary of symbols, or in a dictionary of phrases. Note all the associations, and consider which are used in this chapter.

CONNECT . . .
— Consider how the structures of the game of 'Snakes and Ladders' (described on p. 141) might relate to the events laid out in this chapter. What is the effect of this elaborately extended and playful conceit?

ACCIDENT IN A WASHING-CHEST
SECTION 1 (pp. 149–52)

Focus on: the narrator

EXPLORE THE PARALLEL . . .
— 'My miracle-laden omniscience' (p. 150). In what senses is

an author like a god in the world he creates? And in what senses is he not? Consider Saleem's ironic self-presentation as you read the rest of this chapter.

ACCIDENT IN A WASHING-CHEST
SECTIONS 2–4 (pp. 152–65)

Focus on: fairy tales and archetypal narratives

NOTE AND RELATE . . .
— Carefully read pp. 152–5. Note all the fairy tales and stories drawn from popular culture that are mentioned in this section. What do you know of them? In what ways do these heroes of legends reflect on the characterisation of Saleem and his self-construction in his own narrative?

Focus on: names and naming

REVIEW AND CONSIDER . . .
— Saleem returns to this theme regularly. Consider the expression 'whatsitsname' used by Naseem; or the way Amina is 're-named and so re-invented' (p. 66) when she marries; or the abusive name-calling on pp. 73–7; or the nicknames of Saleem here and on p. 118; or Amina secretly speaking the name of Nadir. Review these, and consider the significance of 'naming' in the novel.

Focus on: washing-chests and dirty laundry

COMPARE . . .
— Refer to Shakespeare's play *The Merry Wives of Windsor* and consider the scene where Falstaff is encouraged to hide in the dirty linen or 'buck' basket in order (supposedly) to escape discovery as the husband of the woman he is wooing is about to

return home. How does Shakespeare's comedy with the idea of the 'dirty laundry' compare with the way it is used in Rushdie's work?

ALL-INDIA RADIO
SECTIONS 1–7 (pp. 165–79)

Focus on: reclaiming the past

READ AND CONSIDER . . .

— 'Does one error invalidate the entire fabric?' (p. 166). Read Rushdie's essay 'Imaginary Homelands' (1992), in which he reflects on writing about India from exile in London: 'If we do look back, we must also do so in the knowledge – which gives rise to profound uncertainties – that our physical alienation means that we will not be capable of reclaiming precisely the thing that was lost; that we will, in short, create fictions, not actual cities or villages, but invisible ones, imaginary homelands, Indias of the mind.' Consider the idea that in trying to reclaim the past we cannot help but create fictions, as it is developed in the novel.

Focus on: narrative technique

DISCUSS . . .

— How is magic realism employed in these sections?

LOVE IN BOMBAY
SECTIONS 1–4 (pp. 180–92)

Focus on: boys and girls

RELATE . . .
— How does this account of the relations between the boys and girls bear on relations between men and women so far in the novel?

MY TENTH BIRTHDAY
SECTION 1 (pp. 192–5)

Focus on: Hindu mythology

RESEARCH . . .
— Although Saleem is a Muslim, he often refers to Hindu mythology. Pick one allusion to Hinduism in this section and do some research to find out its significance. If you are working in a group, present your findings. How is it fitting that Saleem embraces many aspects of Indian culture?

MY TENTH BIRTHDAY
SECTION 2 (pp. 195–200)

Focus on: Midnight's children

IDENTIFY . . .
— The description of Midnight's children resembles a myth. Identify mythical elements in this description. Why have they been presented in these terms, do you think?

MY TENTH BIRTHDAY
SECTIONS 3–5 (pp. 200–7)

Focus on: the narrative 'recipe'

ANALYSE . . .

— Consider how the 'sweet' and 'sour' ingredients of these sections are mixed (and so transformed) by the narrative. If you are unsure of what is meant by this, look ahead to the next exercise.

AT THE PIONEER CAFÉ
SECTIONS 1–6 (pp. 207–22)

Focus on: pickles, mixtures, chutneys

EXPLORE THE METAPHORS . . .

— What is a chutney? If you look up a recipe for chutney, you will see that it is a mixture of sweet and sour ingredients. How could this idea of mixing sweet and sour ingredients that might otherwise be unpalatable (such as green tomatoes), to make something tasty, work as a metaphor for the narrative strategy? A pickle preserves fresh produce, usually in vinegar (wine that has gone sour). Consider the connotations of 'pickle' (such as 'to be in a pickle', 'to be pickled') and of 'vinegar'. Again, explore how the idea of a pickle, which preserves life by transforming it and storing it, might work as a metaphor for this narrative.

Focus on: colours as symbols

NOTE AND ANALYSE . . .

— The Indian national flag, adopted in 1947, is in the colours of deep saffron (the sacred colour of Hinduism, symbolising courage and sacrifice), white (symbolising peace, unity and truth), green (the colour of Islam, symbolising faith and fertility) and blue (symbolising sky and ocean). Which colours are mentioned on pp. 207–13, and in what context? What connotations do these colours have?

ALPHA AND OMEGA
SECTIONS 1–6 (pp. 223–37)

Focus on: self-dramatisation

ANALYSE . . .
— What is the effect of Saleem's self-dramatisation on pp. 229–37?

GAUGE YOUR REACTION . . .
— A character called Rushdie figures fleetingly on p. 233 as a subject of Saleem's envy. The novelist Martin Amis makes the point in his memoir *Experience* (2001, p. 177), referring to his novel *Money* (1984) in which a writer called Martin Amis figures briefly several times, that this joke has the effect of distancing the narrator from the author. How do you react to it?

THE KOLYNOS KID
SECTIONS 1–7 (pp. 237–52)

Focus on: the search for meaning

EVALUATE . . .
— In his search for the meaning of his own life, Saleem makes a case (pp. 237–9) for how his life is a mirror of India's. Analyse his language. How convincing do you find his claims?

Focus on: self-dramatisation

COMMENT . . .
— How do the episodes on pp. 239–252 develop the theme of self-dramatisation?

COMMANDER SABARMATI'S BATON
SECTIONS 1–5 (pp. 252–67)

Focus on: innocence and guilt

SUMMARISE AND DISCUSS . . .
— Look carefully at Saleem's argument with Shiva on pp. 255–6. Summarise both sides of the argument. Whose point of view do you agree with more? Summarise Scharpsteker's advice to Saleem on pp. 256–8. What connotations are evoked by his portrayal as a snake?

TRANSFORM . . .
— The Sabarmati story contains elements of tragedy (the story of a son's revenge for his mother's infidelity recalls Shakespeare's *Hamlet*, for instance, and Saleem behaves with the capriciousness of the gods of ancient Greek tragedy), but more elements of melodrama. Rewrite a scene from this story in high melodramatic style, using the form of a playscript. Which elements lend themselves most easily to this transformation?

REVELATIONS
SECTIONS 1–6 (pp. 267–82)

Focus on: language

ANALYSE . . .
— Analyse the rhetoric of the advertisement on pp. 267–8.

Focus on: the grotesque and the surreal

RESEARCH AND COMMENT . . .
— If you are unfamiliar with the terms 'grotesque' and 'surreal', look them up in the glossary of literary terms. Then comment on Saleem's use of the grotesque and of the surreal in his narrative on pp. 271–8.

Focus on: Revelations

LIST AND COMPARE . . .
— Consider what is meant by a 'revelation'. Look up the strict meaning in a dictionary if you are not sure. In a religious sense, it means the making known of the truth by God (Islam and Christianity both claim to teach the will of God that has been revealed through Prophets, the Quran, or Jesus Christ). In a secular sense, a revelation is the uncovering of a secret. List and compare the various 'revelations' that occur during this chapter.

MOVEMENTS PERFORMED BY PEPPERPOTS
SECTIONS 1–5 (pp. 282–94)

Focus on: stories behind histories

RESEARCH . . .
— This chapter tells an embroidered version of historical

events. Compare Saleem's account of the coup against Mirza with an historical account. You might start by using the website http://www.storyofpakistan.com/

DRAINAGE AND THE DESERT
SECTIONS 1–6 (pp. 294–306)

Focus on: form and intention

CONSIDER . . .

* 'It is possible, even probable, that I am only the first historian to write the story of my undeniably exceptional life-and-times. Those who follow in my footsteps will, however, inevitably come to this present work, the source-book, this Hadith or Purana or *Grundrisse*, for guidance and inspiration' (p. 295).
— Consider how Saleem views the significance of his narrative, and how this determines the kind of narrative he is telling.

JAMILA SINGER
SECTIONS 1–4 (pp. 306–26)

Focus on: smell

STUDY THE METAPHOR . . .
— How is 'smell' used as a metaphor in sections 1–3 (pp. 306–20)?

Focus on: attitudes to women

TRACE AND RELATE . . .
— Look for the various attitudes to women in sections 3–4 (pp. 311–26) and account for them by referring to what you already know of the social context of Indian society.

HOW SALEEM ACHIEVED PURITY
SECTIONS 1–4 (pp. 326–33)

Focus on: narrative strategy

EXAMINE . . .
— Consider the ways in which Saleem creates narrative momentum through a sense of impending arrival in this chapter. How is the fact that Saleem is telling stories about his past (and knows what will happen later) an important aspect of the narrative strategy?

HOW SALEEM ACHIEVED PURITY
SECTIONS 5–7 (pp. 333–44)

Focus on: war

ANALYSE THE ACCOUNT . . .
— Read carefully the description of the Indo-Pakistani war of 1965 in sections 5–7. What is Saleem's 'take' on the war? Compare it with an historical account. What aspects does he emphasise, and how does he link it to his personal narrative? What is the link between violence and purification?

Looking over Book Two

QUESTIONS FOR DISCUSSION OR ESSAYS
✱1. 'Reality is a question of perspective; the further you get from the past, the more concrete and plausible it seems – but as you approach the present, it inevitably seems more and more incredible' (p. 165). Discuss notions of perspective in Book Two.

2. In what ways does Rushdie's use of magic realism liberate his narrative?

3. 'In magic realism there is always a tense connection between the real and the fantastic: the impossible event is a kind of metaphor for the extreme paradoxes of modern history' (David Lodge). Discuss Rushdie's use of magic realism in the light of this comment.

4. Discuss the similarities and contrasts between stories, histories and myths, with reference to Books One and Two.

5. 'What actually happened is less important than what the author can manage to persuade his audience to believe' (pp. 270–1). Discuss the techniques that Rushdie uses to keep alive the reader's scepticism about the truth of Saleem's autobiographical narrative.

6. Discuss the themes of secrets and revelations in Book Two.

7. 'Rushdie presents the political histories of India and Pakistan as unpredictable and chaotic.' Discuss with reference to Book Two.

8. Examine the themes of home and exile in Book Two.

9. Discuss the theme of new beginnings in Book Two.

10. Consider the use of slogans in Book Two.

11. To what extent is *Midnight's Children* a political text? Discuss with reference to Book Two.

BOOK THREE

THE BUDDHA
SECTION 1 (pp. 345–7)

Focus on: images of film

FIND AND EXPLAIN THE METHOD . . .
— On p. 346 you will see two parenthetical passages about film and the movies. Note how many terms are borrowed from the terminology of film techniques. How familiar are you with what they mean and what they look like? How does this series of metaphors help to create a different narrative perspective? Saleem has already used references to cinema in 'At the Pioneer Café'. Note whenever movie analogies appear in the text again.

THE BUDDHA
SECTIONS 2–8 (pp. 347–59)

Focus on: characterisation

ANALYSE . . .
— The boy soldiers Farooq, Ayooba and Shaheed are contrasted with the old man, 'the buddha'. Compare the ways in which the characters are realised. The boys speak a great deal and their words are given in direct speech. What kinds of language do they use?
— The buddha speaks hardly at all and his words are given in indirect speech, relayed by the narrator. How do these techniques affect your views of the characters?

IN THE SUNDARBANS
SECTIONS 1–2 (pp. 360–5)

Focus on: narrative licence

NOTE . . .

— 'My Padma says, "I am happy you ran away"' (p. 360). The 'buddha' is Saleem himself, of course. He, as narrator, keeps denying this and says that he will go on denying it 'until the snake' (p. 360). But in what ways are you continually reminded that this was Saleem? Note down the hints of his characteristics – physical and mental – and note down the 'slips of the tongue' in Saleem's narrative.

Focus on: hallucinations

ANALYSE THE LANGUAGE . . .

— The group, lost in the rain-forest, ill and hungry, start to experience 'the terrible phantasms of the dream-forest' (p. 363). Pick out the words on pp. 362–65 that convey the hallucinatory and dreamlike state. Pick out also repetitious rhymes and assonances that help to convey the character of their state. Look in the glossary of literary terms if you are unsure of the meaning of 'assonance'.

IN THE SUNDARBANS
SECTION 3 (pp. 365–8)

Focus on: listening

RESEARCH AND COMPARE . . .

— On pages 366–7 the group is described hearing voices in the jungle and being maddened by them. The three boys stop their ears with mud, but the 'buddha' goes on listening. Look up the story of Oedipus and the sirens as told in the *Odyssey* of Homer, or in a dictionary of classical myth and legend. How does Odysseus's decision to go on listening to the sirens compare with Saleem's (the 'buddha's') decision? What might this comparison suggest about the 'buddha's' role in this passage, and Saleem's role in the novel as a whole?

Focus on: repetitions and multiples

CONSIDER . . .

— In the Hindu temple the group encounter the four houris. On p. 367 the narrator tells that 'this this this was what they had needed'. How do repetitions in language and imagery help to convey the picture of physical ecstasy?

IN THE SUNDARBANS
SECTIONS 4–6 (pp. 368–73)

Focus on: economy in mourning

ASK YOURSELF . . .

— Ayooba dies, effectively saving Saleem's life. Not much is said about it. How does the sense of loss and grief come across all the same?

RELATE . . .

— Look at the end of the chapter on p. 373. How do the words of Deshmukh, 'the vendor of notions', relate to the themes of the novel as a whole?

SAM AND THE TIGER
SECTION 1 (pp. 374–7)

Focus on: coincidence and the haphazard

REFLECT AND CONNECT . . .

— At the beginning of this chapter we are given a summary of facts and events to do with relations between India and Pakistan in the early 1970s. But the narrator frequently uses terms like 'if . . . I would not . . .', or 'nor, in all likelihood, would . . .'. Other possible outcomes are always being implied. Ask yourself how this sense of contingency applies a) to real experience, and b) to the narrative method of the novel as a whole.

Focus on: mourning

LOOK BACK AND COMPARE . . .

— Shaheed Dar dies on pp. 376–7. Look back at Ayooba's death on pp. 370–1. In what ways are the two scenes similar? What is the effect on you, the reader, of this reminiscence and repetition?

SAM AND THE TIGER
SECTION 2 (pp. 377–9)

Focus on: storytelling

SEARCH AND COMPARE . . .

— 'How the buddha regained his name: Once, long ago . . .' (p. 377). Look at this section and note as many examples as you can find of 'fairy-tale' language or situations. How is the sense of Saleem's narrative being a fairy tale conveyed to you?

What are fairy tales for and who, traditionally, reads them? To find out about fairy tales and their history, you might like to read Marina Warner's books *From the Beast to the Blonde: Fairy Tales and Their Tellers* (1996) and *No Go the Bogeyman: Lulling, Scaring and Making Mock* (1998).

SAM AND THE TIGER
SECTION 3 (pp. 379–80)

Focus on: language, character and stereotypes

ASSESS . . .
— Look at the kinds of phrases used by Sam Manekshaw. How can you tell from his language and vocabulary that he is a stereotyped character?

SAM AND THE TIGER
SECTION 4 (pp. 381–3)

Focus on: the theme of invisibility

SEARCH AND COMPARE . . .
— Saleem is made invisible by Parvati. He compares himself to Haroun al-Rashid. Find out about this medieval Arabic poem (there is a poem on the subject by Alfred Lord Tennyson that might help). What is the point of Saleem's comparison here? In what ways is the narrator of a novel — whether in the first or the third person — always 'invisible'?

THE SHADOW OF THE MOSQUE
SECTION 1 (pp. 384–5)

Focus on: pickles again

RELATE AND TRACE THE ANALOGY . . .

— On pp. 384–5 we are returned to the theme of pickles – storytelling pickles. If you look at the interview with Rushdie on pp. 21–2 you will see that he explains how storytelling, preserving memory, mixing ideas, distilling ingredients, can be compared with the process of pickling and making preserves or chutneys. Look over this section and note down how many words can be applied to pickling and to storytelling.

THE SHADOW OF THE MOSQUE
SECTIONS 2–3 (pp. 385–94)

Focus on: images and idioms

ANALYSE THE METAPHORS . . .

— On p. 391 we are told that Sonia was 'driven certifiably insane by a life in which she had been required to begin "being a chamcha" (literally a spoon, but idiomatically a flatterer)'. Why do you suppose a flatterer is called a 'spoon'? What other terms can you think of for a flatterer? How many similar idiomatic metaphors can you think of? Look out for other examples of this kind of metaphoric application in the novel.

THE SHADOW OF THE MOSQUE
SECTIONS 4–7 (pp. 394–404)

Focus on: history

RESEARCH . . .
— A number of real historical figures are mentioned and described in this chapter. Find out about the political history of India at this time using the events noted in the novel. You might start with the website http://www.kamat.com/kalranga/timeline/timeline.htm and choose 'The rise of the Nehru–Gandhi Family'. Make yourself a history plot to parallel Saleem's fictional plot.

A WEDDING
SECTION 1 (pp. 404–6)

Focus on: narrative structure

LOOK OVER . . .
— This chapter begins (as do many others, but not all) with a section in the narrating present where Saleem thinks over his story and often – but not always – discusses it with Padma. Then he resumes the story. How does this technique of offering a double point of view expand your perspective on the story? Look back over the novel to find other chapters that are introduced in this way, and think again about this question. How do these contemplative sections tend to end? Check on p. 406 for what happens in this instance.

Focus on: too-many-women

RESEARCH THE ALLUSION . . .
— Saleem lists all of the women who have been important

in, or influenced, his life. 'Women and women and women' (p. 405) he says. He goes on to suggest that these many females are all incarnations of an eternal feminine in 'Maya-Shakti mothers' and of the goddess Devi (p. 406). Find out about the goddess Devi in Hindu mythology. You might try the website http://www.asia.si.edu/devi/indextext.htm What does she represent – how many different elements? And how does the fact of her multiplicity reflect on Saleem's meditation on his many mothers? Why is 'Mother India' (p. 404) feminine?

A WEDDING
SECTION 2 (pp. 406–14)

Focus on: comedy and interpretation

COMPARE AND CONTRAST . . .
— On pp. 408–9 we are told of Shiva's exploits with high society ladies; pp. 409–10 tell how the same things happen (the dropped handbags, the secret notes in the sandals) but now – because of the gossiping of Roshanara Shetty – these events seem a humiliation to Shiva, rather than an aggrandisement. How is the comedy of this contrast put across to you? What technical elements (irony, repetition, romantic cliché) make it funny?

A WEDDING
SECTION 3 (pp. 414–15)

Focus on: endings and beginnings

CONSIDER . . .
— Saleem marries Parvati and becomes a father to her child

by Shiva. Why does he comment on 'destiny, inevitably, the antithesis of choice' (p. 415) in relation to these events? Think back over the stories he has told us about his parents and grandparents to assess the comparisons he is making between his own life and theirs.

A WEDDING
SECTION 4 (pp. 415–16)

Focus on: ceremony

RESEARCH . . .
— Find out about the henna ceremony and its significant relation to the marriage ceremony. What other ceremonial activities are mentioned here and what are they designed to promote or convey in the lives of the couple?

A WEDDING
SECTIONS 5–6 (pp. 416–21)

Focus on: public and private

DISCRIMINATE . . .
— On pp. 417–19 Parvati gives birth, while the circumstances of the 'Emergency' give birth to a 'new India' (p. 419). What is significant about the way in which the public and private worlds are juxtaposed? You will see that there is almost no punctuation, and you will also see that the same verbs and adjectives are used for both scenes. Work out which is which and how they might relate to each other.

MIDNIGHT
SECTION 1 (pp. 421–5)

Focus on: narrative approach

CONTRAST . . .

— Saleem offers portentous reflections on the illness of the baby and on the corrupt state of the nation (pp. 422–5). Padma says, 'Just tell what happened, mister!' Whose side are you on?

MIDNIGHT
SECTIONS 2–5 (pp. 425–37)

Focus on: the Ganges

RESEARCH . . .

— Saleem tells us something about the Ganges and the holy city of Benares (p. 432). Find out about the religious significance of the river and consider why it should be that these climactic events take place there.

Focus on: confession

ANALYSE . . .

— Saleem whispers to the wall 'between April and December 1976' (p. 434). Consider the way in which Saleem's 'confession' is given to us. Analyse the words used and the way he speaks. To whom is he speaking? How would you assess the degrees of his 'guilt' and his 'shame'? (p. 434)?

MIDNIGHT
SECTION 6 (p. 437)

Focus on: vocabulary

RESEARCH AND RELATE . . .
— See the various meanings of 'Ectomy' that Saleem lists on p. 437. Look up each term to find out what they mean. How might the 'cutting out' of something relate to the novel as a whole?

MIDNIGHT
SECTION 7–17 (pp. 437–42)

Focus on: plot

ASK YOURSELF . . .
— Are you surprised by the revelation on p. 442 of the changed baby-tags. How significant is this to the plot of the novel as a whole?

ABRACADABRA
SECTION 1 (pp. 443–7)

Focus on: narrative licence

GAUGE YOUR REACTION . . .
— Saleem tells us that he lied about Shiva's death (p. 443). Is this the 'temptation of every autobiographer'? What does this revelation make you feel about the reliability of Saleem's narrative overall? Does it change your attitude to the story you have read?

73

Focus on: too-many-women

CONSIDER AND LOOK BACK . . .
— Durga is introduced on p. 445. Look back at Saleem's reverie on the women in his life on pp. 404–6 and compare this description of Durga with the ideas about women and the feminine expounded in that episode.

ABRACADABRA
SECTIONS 2–3 (pp. 447–52)

Focus on: magic

ANALYSE THE LANGUAGE . . .
— Why is this final chapter called 'Abracadabra'? Look up the derivation of this word in a dictionary. Where does the phrase 'open-sesame' (p. 450) come from? Why do you think that magic and magicians are invoked at the end of this novel?

ABRACADABRA
SECTIONS 4–11 (pp. 452–63)

Focus on: pickles again

ASK YOURSELF AND ANALYSE . . .
— Why does Saleem's story end with the story of Mary Pereira and the chutney factory? How do the final pages of the novel make up a 'chutney'? What is the significance of the 'One empty jar' mentioned on p. 461?

Focus on: *time, and memory*

ASSESS . . .
— Read the final passage on pp. 462–3. How does this section summarise the themes and methods of the novel as a whole? In what ways are time and memory used here, and how do those usages relate to the way they have been emphasised throughout the novel?

Looking over the whole novel

QUESTIONS FOR DISCUSSION OR ESSAYS
1. Discuss the 'commingling of the improbable and the mundane' (p. 9) in *Midnight's Children*.

2. 'There is nothing like a war for the re-invention of lives' (p. 407). Discuss this idea in relation to the novel as a whole.

3. Consider the significance (structurally and metaphorically) of any of the following: the silver spittoon; the perforated sheet; noses and sense of smell; snakes and ladders; pickles and chutneys.

4. Consider the relationship between personal and national fictions in *Midnight's Children*.

5. What does the narrative of *Midnight's Children* say to the reader about the process of narration?

6. 'Scraps, shreds, fragments' (p. 428). In what ways might this phrase epitomise the novel as a whole?

7. What is meant by describing Rushdie as a 'magic realist' author?

8. Discuss the use of symbolism in *Midnight's Children*.

9. Discuss the use of mythology in *Midnight's Children*.

10. Discuss Rushdie's ability to cross cultural and imaginative boundaries.

11. Analyse the treatment of time in *Midnight's Children*.

12. Explore the notions of place and of being 'out of place' in *Midnight's Children*.

13. Consider the idea of 'claiming history' as it is presented in *Midnight's Children*.

14. Discuss the theme of exile in *Midnight's Children*.

15. 'As a people, we are obsessed with correspondences' (p. 300). Discuss the significance of correspondences in *Midnight's Children*.

16. What does Saleem say in *Midnight's Children* about the relationship between what is true and what we believe?

Contexts, comparisons and complementary readings

MIDNIGHT'S CHILDREN

These sections suggest contextual and comparative ways of reading these three novels by Rushdie. You can put your reading in a social, historical or literary context. You can make comparisons – again, social, literary or historical – with other texts or art works. Or you can choose complementary works (of whatever kind) – that is, art works, literary works, social reportage or facts that in some way illuminate the text by sidelights or interventions which you can make into a telling framework. Some of the suggested contexts are directly connected to the book, in that they will give you precise literary or social frames in which to situate the novel. In turn, these are either related to the period within which the novel is set, or to the time – now – when you are reading it. Some of these examples are designed to suggest books or other texts that may make useful sources for comparison (or for complementary purposes) when you are reading *Midnight's Children*, *Shame* or *The Satanic Verses*. Again, they may be related to literary or critical themes, or they may be relevant to social and cultural themes current 'then' or 'now'.

Focus on: the history of India's independence and the history of 'Partition'

SEEK OUT AND READ . . .

India became an independent state at midnight on 15 August 1947. In 1997 the golden jubilee of that date was celebrated. The literary magazine *Granta: The Magazine of New Writing* produced a special issue entitled *India! The Golden Jubilee* (vol. 57, spring 1997) to mark the occasion. This issue includes first-hand accounts from many people about what happened to them on the night of 15 August 1947 and of their attitudes to the process and the fact of independence. It also includes pictures, historical accounts of the events, and a range of new writing from and about India, including work by writers such as Anita Desai, Arundhati Roy, R. K. Narayan, Vikram Seth and V. S. Naipaul. The personal testimonies are of particular interest and give a perspective on the fictional events described in *Midnight's Children*.

— See if you can obtain or borrow a copy. *Granta* is at 2–3 Hanover Yard, Noel Road, London N1 8BE.

RESEARCH . . .

— Research Kashmir, its history and its culture using the World Wide Web. You might try the website at http://www.jammukashmirinfo.com/ Kashmir/

CONSIDER THE LITERARY REPRESENTATION OF HISTORY . . .

— Rushdie's *Midnight's Children* has a specific historical setting and centres on the events surrounding Indian independence in 1947. Compare the ways in which a major historical event is represented in another text. Charles Dickens's *A Tale of Two Cities* (1859) is set during the 1790s in London and Paris while the events of the French Revolution were taking place. In what ways is the treatment of historical events similar in these two novels, and in what ways is it different?

Focus on: elements in the structure of Indian society

RESEARCH . . .

— In the interview Rushdie says that in many ways *Midnight's Children* was about the excess, the 'too muchness', of India. Do some research on the extravagance of India. Find out how many separate Indian states there are. Then find out what kinds of climate exist in the north, in the south, in the east and west. What is the population of each individual state? What is the population of Calcutta, and the population of Bombay? What is the current birth rate in India? How many different kinds of 'caste' are there? How many different religions are followed in India? What different kinds of diet are eaten in different parts of India?

Once you have some of these facts, consider your reading of *Midnight's Children* in their light.

RESEARCH AND CONSIDER . . .

— To research 'the untouchable problem' (p. 293) that is alluded to several times in the novel, do a websearch on 'dalits' or 'untouchables'. How does the information you find there help you to interpret their fictional representation in the novel?

Focus on: the representation of India by the British press

ASSESS . . .

If you have access to the *Times* website find the article entitled 'India call in X-Files agents to unmask face-scratching alien' published on 20 August 2002. It tells about a mysterious flying object seen in the state of Uttar Pradesh said to attack sleeping villagers and nicknamed the *Muhnochwa* (face-scratcher). What impression of Indian culture does this article emphasise?

Focus on: narrative, genre and authorial commentary

RESEARCH AND COMPARE . . .

— In Rushdie's collection *Imaginary Homelands: Essays and Criticism 1981–1991* (1991: Penguin, London, 1992) the three opening essays consider the idea of memory in *Midnight's Children*, the technique of unreliable narration in the novel, and the central premise of Saleem (and Rushdie himself) being born at the time of India's independence. Read these essays and consider how they assist in your own reading of *Midnight's Children*.

Focus on: narrative, and the real and the surreal

COMPARE . . .

— If you look at the interview with Salman Rushdie you will see that he cites the works of Charles Dickens (1812–1870) as one of the influences on his style. In particular Rushdie says, 'Dickens manages to pull off the trick of having an incredibly meticulously naturalistically observed background, and then to project against that a completely surrealistic foreground (p. 30).' Read any one of Dickens's novels to compare Rushdie's technique with his. In particular you might like to look at the opening passage of *Bleak House* (1852–3) where a 'realist' account of the filthy and foggy streets of nineteenth-century London is juxtaposed with a surreal fantasy of a prehistoric vision.

RESEARCH AND COMPARE . . .

— Another influential writer that Rushdie mentions is Laurence Sterne (1713–1768), the author of *The Life and Opinions of Tristram Shandy* (1759–67). Told in a haphazard rambling manner with many digressions and delays, the hero – like

Saleem Sinai – spends a large part of the narrative not managing to get born, or even – for some time – conceived. Read all or part of *Tristram Shandy* to see how this delaying tactic in dealing with time has been exploited by Rushdie.

COMPARE . . .
— Read Rushdie's book of short stories for children called *Haroun and the Sea of Stories* (1991). How do the themes played out in these stories connect to the themes of *Midnight's Children?*

Focus on: Bollywood

RESEARCH . . .
The Bombay film industry has been a major influence on Indian culture. Nicknamed 'Bollywood', the studios work in the old-fashioned Hollywood mould – making films on set or using extravagant locations, having a 'stable' of popular acting stars who are contracted for a certain number of films, who are often typecast, and who develop a wide and passionate following. The formula for a typical 'Bollywood' film is the tale of young lovers thrown together by circumstances, then cruelly torn apart only to be reunited in the last reel. Stock characters might include the nagging mother, the villainous uncle, and the conniving marriage arranger. But the consistent key feature is the use of songs and extended song-and-dance sequences involving a cast of hundreds. In recent years this style of movie – once very much a home-grown product and to be seen only in India – has developed a wider appeal. The well-known writer of musicals Andrew Lloyd Webber has turned his hand to the trade to produce *Bollywood Dreams*, and smash hits such as *The Guru* (2002) have been a big box-office draw.
— In all of his novels Rushdie has employed the film language of Bollywood as well as a play on the typical film narratives

that are to be encountered there. Look through *Midnight's Children* for the places where Rushdie uses a film framework. Go and see a Bollywood film to see how the formula relates to Rushdie's literary work. And if you want to find out more about Rushdie and his ideas about and attitudes to film, then read his book on the cinema called *The Wizard of Oz* (1992).

READ AND CONSIDER . . .

— During the 1990s the BBC considered — and began work on — a television adaptation of Rushdie's *Midnight's Children*. Rushdie himself eventually wrote the script for this adaptation and it is published by Vintage (1999) though the film was, in the end, never made. Read Rushdie's account of the process of the adaptation. In particular consider the passages where he speaks about his own sense of freedom in adapting the novel to another form and the ways in which he went about cutting and condensing. Then read the screenplay and consider the ways in which the novel has been adapted into this new form. How do the two compare in your opinion?

Focus on: history and theory

LOOK AHEAD . . .

See also pp. 164–5 for suggested contextual reading on 'colonial', 'post-colonial' and the interventions of critical theory.

VINTAGE
LIVING
TEXTS

Shame
IN CLOSE-UP

Reading guides for

SHAME

BEFORE YOU BEGIN TO READ . . .
— Look at the interview with Rushdie. You will see there that he identifies a number of themes:

- Childhood
- Multiplicity
- The idea of history
- The presence of the reader
- The hero on the periphery

Other themes that may be useful to consider while reading the novel include:

- Shame and being ashamed
- Absence and presence
- Storytelling
- Parents and children
- Fairy stories
- Partition

Reading activities: detailed analysis

THE TITLE

CONSIDER . . .

— Think about the meaning of the title. Write down all the meanings that the word 'shame' might convey to you. Keep a note of this and consult it whenever you meet the word 'shame' or to be 'ashamed' in the course of your reading. If you encounter a meaning not already on your list, add it.

THE CHAPTER HEADINGS

ASSESS . . .

— Look carefully at the chapter headings and the headings for the five sections of the book. Then let your mind wander and think about what sort of a world it might be that is conjured up by these headings. Is it a world of soap opera? A world of factual history? A scientific world? A realistic documentary world? If none of these, then what?

THE FAMILY TREE
(p. 10)

EXAMINE AND ASK YOURSELF . . .
— Look at the family tree. Does it help you to get an idea of what might be offered you as you start to read? Family trees are usually to be found in serious books – history books on royal families for instance. How serious is this family tree? What here might make you suspicious?

PART I: ESCAPES FROM THE MOTHER COUNTRY

CHAPTER ONE
(pp. 11–25)

Focus on: fairy tales

CONSIDER . . .
— What kind of world is this? What elements might suggest that this is a fable or a fairy tale? List the words or the circumstances that suggest some 'magical' setting.

Focus on: fairy tales and threes

COMPARE . . .
— Read Angela Carter's short story 'The Snow Child' from the collection *The Bloody Chamber* (1979) and read Jeanette Winterson's short story 'The Three Friends' from the collection *The World and Other Places* (1997). Both of these stories use the idea of three, and here in *Shame* we meet three sisters. What is the significance of the number? What other things might it suggest to you – in religious life or in social life, in family life,

or in geometry? Why might three be considered a 'magic' number? How many other stories can you think of that begin with 'There were once three —s . . .'?

Focus on: vocabulary

LOOK UP . . .

— Note down all the strange words in this chapter and then look them up in a dictionary if you don't already know their meaning. Examples might include 'maidan', 'Cantonment', 'zenana', 'Hegiran'. Then ask yourself a) what kind of world does this conjure up? And b) what literary effect is achieved by the inclusion of so many – probably strange – words?

Focus on: Omar Khayyam

RESEARCH . . .

— The son born to these three mothers on p. 20 is called Omar Khayyam. What does this name mean to you? Research who he was and why he is well known. When you have found that out, consider what this knowledge adds to your expectation of the text.

ASK YOURSELF . . .

— 'Dizzy, peripheral, inverted, infatuated, insomniac, stargazing, fat: what manner of hero is this?' (p. 25). Think about the heroes of literature. Are they traditionally 'stargazing' types? 'Dizzy'? 'Peripheral'? and what about 'fat'? What kind of a hero do you think this is?

CHAPTER TWO
(pp. 26–43)

Focus on: structures

CONSIDER . . .

— Read the section on pp. 26–7 where the 'procedures' for building a house in the 'Defence' area of the city are described. The rules – in themselves – might make sense, but the piling up of different rules begins to make the situation absurd, and yet – at the same time – everyone accepts them and works round them. Can you think of other circumstances or stories where the ways in which we accept conventions and structures is satirised? You might look at the account of the Circumlocution Office in Chapter Ten of the first book of Charles Dickens's *Little Dorrit* (1855–7) or of the workings of the Court of Chancery in the opening chapters of his *Bleak House* (1852–3). Another example might be the story of 'The Emperor's New Clothes'. Look up the story if you do not know it and relate the circumstances there to what is happening here. Or you might think about the rules at your school, or the rules at your place of work – if there are any. How sensible are they? Can they be interpreted as absurd? In what ways might these social structures resemble the structures of narrative fiction?

Focus on: the theme of shame

NOTE DOWN . . .

— The word 'shame' is mentioned several times in this chapter. Note down each occasion and each particularised meaning and add it to the collection you are making.

Focus on: the narrator

ASK YOURSELF . . .

— Who is telling this story? 'I' appears on p. 26 to tell us various stories about himself, his family, his friends and his historical circumstances. Collect as much information on the narrator as you can as you read through the novel (there isn't much), and assess a) his perspective, and b) his manipulation of the reader. What do you suppose he means by telling us 'I, too, am a translated man' (p. 29)? How might the fact of that 'translation' be colouring his attitudes to the telling of this story?

Focus on: vocabulary

LIST, RESEARCH AND COMPARE . . .

— Read the passage describing the three sisters' house on p. 30. List every word that conveys decay of any kind. What is the cumulative effect of this picture and use of imagery? Then look up Chapter Eight of volume I of Charles Dickens's *Great Expectations* (1860–1) where the boy Pip first visits Miss Havisham. In what ways is Rushdie's vocabulary similar to that of Dickens? How helpful is the comparison between the three sisters and Miss Havisham? In what ways might their fugitive enterprises be the same?

Focus on: allusion and reference

RESEARCH AND COMPARE . . .

— Omar Khayyam describes himself to Farah as a wolf child, though Farah tells him he is no 'jungle-boy'. What do you know about 'wolf children'? How many examples can you think of? Look up as many such stories as you can. They might include Romulus and Remus, the story of Kaspar Hauser, Mowgli the jungle boy, Tarzan. You will be able to find others. When you have some examples, consider what the myth suggests about the relationship between nature and nurture, between the natural and the civilised, between the wild and the tamed. Ask yourself and your friends and debate how far this comparison may be related to questions of innocence versus experience.

RESEARCH AND COMPARE . . .

— Read the passage on Omar Khayyam's mothers on p. 40, from 'And there is an even stranger matter to report' to 'no doubt because it was marinated in bile'. Then look at the description of the older Flora Finching – as opposed to the younger Flora – in Chapter Thirteen of Charles Dickens's *Little Dorrit*, (1855–6) where the narrator describes how Flora has become a 'moral mermaid' with her older, socially clod-hopping self grafted on to her coy and charmingly giggly younger self. How does comparison with this passage in Dickens help you to read the similar account of psychological mismatches in *Shame*?

CHAPTER THREE
(pp. 44–56)

Focus on: the theme of looking and the gaze

NOTE AND CONSIDER . . .

— Omar possesses a telescope and is described as a 'voyeur'. Look through this chapter and note as many references as you can to the theme of looking or peeping or examining or scrutinising. Consider the various meanings of the gaze. Think about who is being looked at and by whom and for what purpose. Is it relevant that Farah's perspective on Omar is occasionally included here? What does 'perspective' mean? Look also at the passage on pp. 51–2 where Omar and Farah visit the border post. How are the broken shards of mirror relevant to this theme? Note especially how this paragraph ends. What might any of this – both literally and metaphorically – have to do with the fact that Omar Khayyam is an expert hypnotist?

Looking over Part I

QUESTIONS FOR DISCUSSION OR ESSAYS

1.   'But shame is like everything else; live with it for long enough and it becomes part of the furniture' (p. 28). Discuss, in relation to the events and the themes of Part I.

2.   Why is this section set in 'the fourteenth century' (p. 13)?

3.   Consider the characterisation of Omar and Farah so far.

4.   Look at the story of the narrator's friend the poet on pp. 27–8. How does this story relate the themes of Part I as a whole?

5.   'The country in this story is not Pakistan, or not quite. There are two countries, real and fictional, occupying the same space, or almost the same space. My story, my fictional country exists, like myself, at a slight angle to reality. I have found this off-centring to be necessary; but its value is, of course, open to debate' (p. 29). Discuss, in relation to either the setting or the narrative method of Part I.

PART II: THE DUELLISTS

CHAPTER FOUR
(pp. 59–71)

Focus on: Sufiya Zinobia

COMPARE . . .

— We are told on p. 59 that 'This is a novel about Sufiya Zinobia', and yet the end of the chapter she still has not been born. If you have read Rushdie's *Midnight's Children*, consider how Sufiya Zinobia's introduction is similar to that of Saleem Sinai.

Focus on: realism, fairy tale and satire

LOOK UP AND ANALYSE . . .

— Look up the terms 'realism', 'fairy tale' and 'satire' in the glossary of literary terms. On pp. 68–71 the narrator discusses with himself – and with us – the question of what kind of novel it is that he is writing. 'If this were a realistic novel about Pakistan,' he begins. Then he says, 'But suppose this were a realistic novel!', and he concludes with two thoughts: 'Realism can break a writer's heart' and 'Fortunately, however, I am only telling a sort of modern fairy-tale, so that's all right'. How does this narrator treat realism? And fairy tale? How satirical is his account on pp. 69–70 about the *real* events in Pakistan that he would have to include if this were a 'realistic' novel? In what ways might this be, after all, a 'realistic novel'?

CHAPTER FIVE
(pp. 72–90)

Focus on: extended imagery

OUTLINE . . .
— Look at the passage on p. 74 which begins, '"See if we don't have sons," Raza told Bilquìs, "In my mother's family boys grow on trees."' How many words and images in the sentences that follow on immediately from this pick up the imagery of the 'tree'. If you look back at p. 63 at the paragraph beginning 'Don't ask who planted the bomb', you will see that the narrative does something similar with 'seeds' and 'plants', etc. What is the effect of this extended imagery? Is it absurd, pleasing, revealing? There are several other examples of this technique in this chapter and throughout the book. Look out for them and consider their effect and their significance.

CHAPTER SIX
(pp. 91–112)

Focus on: the theme of shame and the theme of honour

CONSIDER . . .
— Look back over your notes on what kinds of 'shame' there may be. Consider how they might be connected to the theme of honour. How are the two connected in the minds of the perpetrators of the events told in this chapter?

Focus on: narrative structure

TRACE . . .
— The chapter begins with the saying about 'the frog who

95

croaks in the shaft of a well' (p. 91). Look for other references to this proverb and show how the narrative is being structured around the saying.

NOTE . . .
— 'Life is long,' says Iskander Harappa on p. 98. Remember this phrase. Look out for it – and versions of it – as you read.

Focus on: untranslatable words

CRITICALLY EVALUATE . . .
— Read the passage on p. 104 about *takallouf*, an untranslatable word, and a particular and refined concept about communication. Consider the proposition that some words are 'untranslatable'. Can you think of any? In particular think about concepts that are peculiar to one group of people or to social settings or situations. How do 'untranslatable' words bind the group and alienate those who are not of the group?

Looking over Part II

QUESTIONS FOR DISCUSSION OR ESSAYS
1. What does Sufiya Zinobia represent so far in the novel?

2. In what ways is Omar Khayyam's role as a 'man on the periphery' been developed in this section?

3. Can you explain the point of the joke on p. 112 in relation to the themes of this section as a whole?

4. Analyse the narrative structure of the novel so far.

5. What is the significance of Rani's embroidery?

PART III: SHAME, GOOD NEWS AND THE VIRGIN

CHAPTER SEVEN
(pp. 115–45)

Focus on: the theme of shame

DEFINE AND ASSESS . . .

— This section opens with a long passage reflecting on the character of 'shame', honour, dishonour, shamelessness, dispossession and pride. Consider, first of all, the stories told about real events in the opening passages of the chapter. How do you react to the events outlined there? What new definitions of 'shame' do they help to add? How do these stories and the 'morals of these stories' relate to the concerns of the novel as a whole?

TRACE AND ACCOUNT FOR . . .

— Look through at the words used to describe Sufiya's 'blushing' and the associated connotations of redness, heat, sacrifice and burning. Note down as many examples of this linked vocabulary as you can. Why, in the light of the way that Sufiya Zinobia is being used, do they raise relevant terms and images? Think particularly of the circumstances in which people use fire, and think also of occasions where people – whether alive or dead – have been burned in history, or in current-day events.

CHAPTER EIGHT
(pp. 146–73)

Focus on: fairy tales, allusion and reference

COMMENT ON . . .

— The title of this chapter is 'Beauty and the Beast'. If you don't know the fairy tale already, then look it up. Look back at p. 139 where 'the beast inside the beauty' is mentioned. Then look through the whole of this chapter for references to this fairy tale, or to any other legends and fairy tales. In particular, consult the passage on p. 158 where the narrator's friend explains and interprets the fable of Beauty and the Beast. Then consider what 'the beast inside the beauty' may mean and how the story relates to the inversion.

Looking over Part III

QUESTION FOR DISCUSSION OR ESSAYS

Consider ANY ONE of these quotations in the light of this section, and in relation to the themes of the novel so far:

● 'History is natural selection' (p. 124).
● 'What is a saint? A saint is a person who suffers in our stead' (p. 141).
● 'A city is a camp for refugees' (p. 145).

PART IV: IN THE FIFTEENTH CENTURY

CHAPTER NINE
(pp. 177–96)

Focus on: key sayings

CRITICALLY EVALUATE . . .

— Note the number of phrases in this chapter which are set in small capitals or in italics: phrases like 'A NEW MAN FOR A NEW CENTURY' (p. 177), or '*Rough justice . . . but justice all the same*' (p. 179). Write each of these phrases out as you come to them and assess their value and relation to the chapter and to the novel as a whole.

Focus on: 'clairvoyance' and irony

DECIDE . . .

— On p. 184 we are told a story about Talvar Ulhaq's 'clairvoyance' and his ability to read what criminals are up to before they have even committed the crime. What do you make of this? Can he really see into the future? How does irony work in this passage?

Focus on: xenophobic jokes

ASK YOURSELF . . .

— Iskander plays jokes on the international ambassadors by working with their national stereotypes. How does this short episode relate to the themes of the novel as a whole? Also, ask yourself how many xenophobic jokes you can think of. What do they suggest about the attitudes of one country or group to another?

Focus on: the image of the embroidered shawl

RESEARCH . . .

— Rani's many embroidered shawls tell the various stories of her husband's crimes. Do some research and see what you can find out about places where weaving or embroidery was used to tell some important tale, and then compare those legendary or historical circumstances with those that surround Rani. Examples that you could look for include the story of Penelope or the story of Philomela in Greek legend, the story of the Norns in the Ring Cycle, the story of the Bayeux tapestry.

Focus on: narrative structure

LOOK BACK AND LOOK FORWARD . . .

— Read the passage on p. 187 about Iskander's death and the return of his body to his wife. Then look forward to p. 238 where we are told the same story of the same episode again, but with more detail and from a different perspective. Consider how many times Rushdie (or his narrator) has used the same technique so far in the novel. How many times have you had to look back to find a — slightly different — account of an episode you have already heard about? What effect does this have on your attitude to the text and your reactions to events and characters?

CHAPTER TEN
(pp. 197–220)

Focus on: narrative structure

LOOK BACK . . .

— On pp. 198–9 Bilquìs attempts to explain to Sufiya Zinobia the facts of events on her forthcoming wedding day. Think

back over the story of the novel so far and work out the connections that are there in Sufiya's claim 'I hate fish' (p. 199),
and her voice being that of the 'disguised voice of the latent
monster' (p. 199).

— How many such narrative connections can you make
between events and images described in this chapter and events
and images that have gone before?

CHAPTER ELEVEN
(pp. 221–39)

Focus on: allusion and reference

RESEARCH AND COMPARE . . .

— On p. 239 we are given a quotation from a play called *The
Suicide* by the Russian writer Nikolai Erdman: 'Only the dead
can say what the living are thinking.' How does this relate to
the title of the chapter? How might it relate to the themes of
the novel as a whole? How does it relate to the narrative structure? Think especially about the way in which we are told the
bare facts of Iskander's death on p. 187, only to have many
more circumstances about that death filled in throughout the
course of this chapter.

CHAPTER TWELVE
(pp. 240–63)

Focus on: the figure of the narrator and narrative structure

TO WHAT EXTENT? . . .

— How does this opening passage of this chapter – set in
London and concerned with an account of the narrator's visit

to a production of *Danton's Death* (pp. 240–2) – connect to the
themes of the novel as a whole?

— Look at the short passage on p. 241, '. . . and I am reminded
of a British diplomat's wife whom I mentioned earlier'. Do
you remember this incident? If not, you will find it on page
29. How does the British diplomat's wife's remark help to illustrate the themes of the novel?

Focus on: allusion and reference

GUESS . . .

— Who is the 'ancient writer with a rather martial name'
(p. 241)? A clue: he is the author of *Julius Caesar*.

Focus on: allusion and political irony

RESEARCH AND COMPARE . . .

— Read the passage on p. 245 that forms the central section
from 'General Hyder' to 'They must be some other thing.' How
ironic is this statement of political practice? Then ask yourself
the same questions about the passage on pp. 249–50 beginning
'Two years after the death of Iskander Harappa' to 'underes-
timated your skills', and also the long narrative aside on pp. 250–1
from 'May I interpose a few words here' to 'I recommend them
highly.'

— Do you recognise the phrase 'liberty, equality, fraternity'?
If not, then look it up. How ironic is its use here? Why might
the narrator refer to these terms as three 'myths'?

— On p. 251 the narrative mentions that Pakistan and Israel
were two theocracies, with Iran under the reign of the mul-
lahs being a third. Look up the term 'theocracy'. What does it
mean? How are theocracies portrayed in the novel as a whole?
To compare the fictional state described in *Shame* with another
fictional theocracy, read Margaret Atwood's novel *The
Handmaid's Tale* (1985). What elements are similar in the rules

and conventions that obtain in both states portrayed in these two books?

Looking over Part IV

QUESTIONS FOR DISCUSSION OR ESSAYS

1. 'Human beings have a remarkable talent for persuading themselves of the authenticity and nobility of aspects of themselves which are in fact expedient, spurious, base' (p. 198). Discuss, in relation to the actions of one or two of the characters in *Shame*.

2. 'Well, well, I mustn't forget I'm only telling a fairy-story' (p. 257). In what ways does the narrator of *Shame* forget that he's telling a fairy story?

3. What do you suppose Sufiya Zinobia represents in this section? Why does she disappear?

PART V: JUDGMENT DAY
(pp. 267–86)

Focus on: foreground and background

ASSESS . . .

— 'It is almost over' (p. 267); 'Stories end, worlds end; and then it's judgment day' (pp. 276–7). The foreground story in this last section of the novel tells how Omar Khayyam Shakil took Bilquìs and Raza back to the home of his mothers and how they died there. The background story wraps up all the other stories of the novel – including giving us stories like that of Omar's great-grandfather and his brother (pp. 277–8). How do the foreground and the background here relate to each other?

Focus on: Sufiya Zinobia

ANALYSE . . .

— Explain the symbolic role played by the figure of Sufiya Zinobia in this last section and in the novel as a whole.

Looking over the whole novel

QUESTIONS FOR DISCUSSION OR ESSAYS

1.   'This is a novel about Sufiya Zinobia [. . .] Or perhaps it would be more accurate, if also more opaque, to say that Sufiya Zinobia is about this novel' (p. 59). Now that you have read the whole novel, relate these statements to your view of the book as a whole.

2.   Explain which elements of *Shame* can be characterised as 'realist' and which are 'fantastic'.

3.   Illustrate the range of points of view enlisted in *Shame* and explain how each illuminates the others.

4.   Describe the character of the narrative persona in *Shame*.

5.   How does the circular narrative structure of *Shame* – beginning and ending in the same house – contribute to the themes and concerns of the novel?

6.   'There is no country poorer than Escape' (p. 267). Discuss, in relation to the novel as a whole.

Contexts, comparisons and complementary readings

SHAME

Focus on: history

RESEARCH AND COMPARE . . .

— *Shame* is set in an imaginary country that is and is not Pakistan and it retells the history of events that took place there in the late twentieth century when President Zulfikar Ali Bhutto was deposed and then murdered by General Zia Ul-Haq. Find out about these events. You might look at the website http://www.countryreports.org/history/pakishist.htm

— Read the two articles by Rushdie 'Zia Ul-Haq, 17 August 1988' and 'Daughter of the East' (a review of a book by Bhutto's daughter Benazir, herself later President of Pakistan). They are included in his collection *Imaginary Homelands: Essays and Criticism 1981–1991* (1991: Granta and Penguin, London, 1992).

— Consider his portrayal of the fictional events in *Shame* in the light of the comments and attitudes revealed in these essays.

Focus on: the theme of shame

RESEARCH AND CONSIDER . . .

— Look up the word 'shame' in a dictionary, preferably the *Oxford English Dictionary*. How many different meanings and contexts can you find for the concept? Then look up the word in a Thesaurus. How does this help you to define its many meanings?

— Then read this article taken from *The Times* about an event in Pakistan in 2002. What connotations does 'shame' have for the people to whom these things happened? Think about the 'shame' of the daughter who was gang-raped, the 'shame' of the woman who allegedly had an affair with the twelve-year-old boy, the 'shame' of the sodomised boy, and the 'shame' of the father of the two young people attacked by the rival clan.

Six to be hanged for Pakistan gang rape
From Zahid Hussain in Islamabad

The Pakistani woman victim of a gang rape was in fear of her life yesterday after a special court sentenced to death by hanging four rapists and two members of a village jury that authorised the crime.

The victim, Mai Mukhtaran, said that her family planned to quit their village in southern Punjab after threats of reprisals by the attackers' clan.

Hundreds waited for hours outside a heavily guarded court in Dera Ghjazi Khan for the verdicts in a trial that had horrified the nation and had been closely watched by international human rights groups.

Judge Zulfiquar Ali Malik's verdict was announced soon after midnight in his chambers with all 14 defendants present. Those receiving the death sentence included four accused of the rape and two members of a tribal council that ordered the June 22 assault in the village of Meerawali. They were also fined £400 each. The eight who were acquitted were members of the council.

A defence lawyer said that he would challenge the conviction in the High Court within seven days. It is the first time in Pakistan that rapists have been sentenced to death.

Human rights groups have called for the banning of the tribal councils that dominate tribal regions and demanded enforcement of stringent laws to stop crimes against women.

Ms Mai, 30, did not go to the court but stayed in her village home. 'I waited till one in the morning. My elder brother had gone to the court, but he had not yet returned and we were really upset. I was so tired by then, I fell asleep. Then at 2.30am my father woke me up. I saw many policemen inside my home and they all were congratulating us. I felt elated and I immediately threw my hands towards the sky and said, "Thank you Allah. Justice is delivered."'

Her brother, Hazoor Baksh, who with other relations stood outside the court under police guard, said: 'I am satisfied the judge has done justice for us.'

Police increased security around the Meerawali home of Ms Mai, who said she was receiving death threats. 'Not only my family, but those who supported us are being threatened with dire consequences. They have told us they would kill our men.' She has asked the Government for a house in a safer place.

Ms Mai, a member of the socially low Gujar clan, was gang-raped by four men on June 22 on a tribal council's orders as a punishment for an alleged sexual affair that her 12-year-old brother had with a 25-year-old woman of the rival Mastoi clan. She was made to walk home in tattered clothes amid the jeers and laughter from more than 500 villagers. Members of the Mastoi clan also sodomised her brother. The council ordered that he should marry the woman with whom he was linked.

Ms Mai said that the Mastoi clan had fabricated the story against her brother to cover up its own crime. Her family did not report the incident to the police because of fear of reprisals. Officials acted after local newspapers reported the crime. The outcry forced the military regime to order a trial in a summary court, and the authorities offered the family compensation.

Gang rapes are often used to avenge family honour and 'honour' killings of women are not uncommon in rural areas of the country.

COMPARE . . .

— Look at some other literary texts that deal with concepts of 'shame'.

— You might look at Shakespeare's play *Titus Andronicus* and consider how Lavinia's rape and mutilation brings 'shame' on her father and her family. Ask yourself what kind of 'shame' this may be.

— Or else look at the opening chapters of Charles Dickens's *Bleak House* (1852–3) where the upbringing of Esther Summerson is described as she is constantly scolded and belittled by her aunt and reminded of the 'shame' of her illegitimate birth.

— Then look at William Golding's novel *Rites of Passage* (1985). In this novel something happens to the parson called Collins during a voyage on board a ship bound for Australia. It takes some time to work out what that something is — so persist, and look for the clue at the end which is not about chewing tobacco. The parson clearly considers himself 'shamed' and seems to allow himself to die because of self-disgust. We are told that he writes that only what a man does can defile him.

— Think about concepts of 'shame' in terms of what others do to you, and what you do yourself. How do these different focuses affect your reading of the theme in Salman Rushdie's novel?

— You might also like to look at J. M. Coetzee's novel *Disgrace* (1999). How is the theme of 'shame' — whether self-inflicted or not — played out there, and how do Coetzee's ideas compare with Rushdie's take on the subject?

Focus on: allusion and reference to legend and fairy tale

RESEARCH, LIST, COMPARE AND ASSESS . . .

— There is a strand in *Shame* which uses a great number of fairy-tale plots and methods. Consider the beginning with the three sisters shut up in their tower. What might this remind you of? *Sleeping Beauty*? The legend of Danae? *Rapunzel*? How many others can you think of?

Other examples might include the stories of the *Ring* cycle, where Harappa's daughter, with her nickname of 'virgin iron-pants', might become a version of Brünhilde, the Valkyrie, warrior daughter of Wotan, chief of the Norse gods. Or else Rani's embroidered shawls which tell stories might be compared with the Norns — or Fates — weaving the threads of destiny. Otherwise she might be compared with Philomela telling the story of her rape and mutilation by Tereus by weaving the story into a tapestry. Or with Penelope, waiting for the return of her husband Odysseus and yet besieged by suitors to whom she has made the promise that she will make her choice once her tapestry is done – tapestry which she works on every day, only to unravel it at night.

— Work through *Shame* and note down as many comparisons as you can think of and list them. Then consider a) what moral or cultural 'lesson' is being offered by the fairy stories you have collected, and b) in what ways is Rushdie's text expanding on or revising those social or cultural expectations?

VINTAGE
LIVING
TEXTS

The Satanic Verses

IN CLOSE-UP

Reading guides for

THE SATANIC VERSES

BEFORE YOU BEGIN TO READ . . .
— Look at the interview with Rushdie. You will see there that he identifies a number of themes:

- Forgiveness and reconciliation
- The seen and the unseen
- Love
- Magic realism, realism, naturalism
- Death

Other themes and ideas that may be useful to consider while reading the novel include:

- Belief and religion
- Intertextuality
- The author as reader
- Jazz, improvisation and music as a literary analogy
- The city

Reading activities: detailed analysis

CONTENTS

Look at the Contents page. How many of these headings suggest a focus on the supernatural or the miraculous? What can you tell about the novel and its themes from these headings?

EPIGRAPH

Read the epigraph, which is a quotation from Daniel Defoe's *The History of the Devil*. Note that, even in this quotation, there is mention of Satan's 'angelic nature'. Do some research about the history of the devil. Read the book of Genesis in the Bible. Lucifer was once an angel who disobeyed God and was thrown out of heaven as a result. You might also like to read John Milton's *Paradise Lost* (1667) – a famous and important reworking of this story. Consider the implications of the fact that the devil was – to begin with – an angel. Find out as much as you can about the perception of devils and angels in different cultures.

PART 1: THE ANGEL GIBREEL

CHAPTER 1
(pp. 3–10)

Focus on: the idea of the fall

CONSIDER . . .

— Gibreel Farishta and Saladin Chamcha fall out of the skies. Consider the image and the metaphor of 'the fall'. What is 'the Fall of Man'? What is a 'fallen woman'? Can you think of examples in literature or art or history where the fall is more than just the fact of someone falling off a cliff or a building? You might consider the fall of Lucifer; the supposed suicide of the ancient Greek poet Sappho; the fall of Louisa Musgrove on the steps of the Cobb at Lyme Regis in Jane Austen's *Persuasion* (1818); the fall of Floria Tosca at the end of Giacomo Puccini's opera *Tosca* (1900); the fall from a bridge in François Truffaut's film *Jules et Jim* (1961); the fall from a cliff in Nicholas Ray's *Rebel Without a Cause* (1955).

— Now link whatever falls you have managed to collect with the fall of Gibreel and Saladin. In what ways does Gibreel's phrase 'To be born again first you have to die' connect with other images of the fall?

Focus on: the images of destruction and creation

WRITE DOWN AND COUNT UP . . .

— How many instances can you find here of references to either birth or death? How is each one related to the other in this passage? What does it suggest about the rhythms and cycles of destruction and creation?

Focus on: colour

WRITE DOWN AND COUNT UP . . .
— Note any mention of colour that you come across in the
chapter. How many of these references are to colour? And
which colours? How many are to shades of white? Remember
these allusions – you will need them later.

Focus on: the theme of revelation

NOTE . . .
— 'Slow down; you think Creation happens in a rush? So
then, neither does revelation . . .' (p. 5). If you consult the Bible
you will see that the first book is called 'Genesis' and the last
book is called 'Revelation'. Look up both of these words and
find out their strict meanings. How might the themes of creation and revelation connect to the idea of writing a novel?
What is being created? What is being revealed?

Focus on: names

WORK OUT . . .
— Gibreel is a version of the word Gabriel in English.
'Farishta' means 'angel' in Urdu. What does this name suggest
about Gibreel's role?
— And why is Saladin's surname 'Chamcha'? Find out what
the word means in Hindi. If you have read – or if you read
– Salman Rushdie's *Midnight's Children* (p. 391) you will find part
of the answer. And what about 'Saladin'? Look up the name
in a dictionary of mythology and see how many famous
Saladins you can find.

PART I, CHAPTER 2
(pp. 11–32)

Focus on: centres and margins

LIST . . .

— Work through this chapter and separate out which section relates to which bit of the story. There is the tale of Gibreel's life as a film star; the story of his parentage and his growing up; there is mention of his immediate past as he left Bombay; there is the episode of his being aboard the aircraft that has been blown up by the terrorists. How many other stories are there in here? And which is presently at the centre, and which are – presently – on the margins? When you have your list you will be able to come back to it to sort out the framework when – as will happen – one story or another moves from the centre to the margins – and vice versa. Consider what the effects are of this technique on your attitudes to the text.

Focus on: language and image

LOOK FOR . . .

— One of Rushdie's literary techniques is the building up and extending of an image. On p. 11, for instance, he builds around the idea of 'illness' to add in 'Germs', and 'Malaise' and 'Bug'. On p. 13 there are a number of references to bad smells and to noses. Whenever you come across a little cluster of images like this, note how they construct a tiny narrative of their own and consider what contribution this method makes to the tone of the novel as a whole.

Focus on: the image of the fall

LOOK BACK AND ADD . . .

— Look over the thoughts you have had about the idea of

the 'fall'. Now think about the fact that Rekha Merchant killed herself by throwing herself and her children from the roof of her high-rise home. Why is it called 'Everest Vilas'? And what do you make of the headlines that announced her demise as instanced on p. 15?

Focus on: colour

LOOK BACK . . .
— You have already begun to note down the use of colour imagery in *The Satanic Verses*. Remember that white is especially important. First of all, look for the places where white and related colours appear in this chapter. Then ask yourself what the colour white 'means'. What does it symbolise? Who wears white? When do people wear white? With whom is it associated? Bear all these images in mind as you carry on with your reading.

PART I, CHAPTER 3
SECTIONS 1–5 (pp. 33–46)

Focus on: stories, myths, intertexts and reference

COMMENT ON . . .
— 'Once upon a time – *it was and it was not so*, as the old stories used to say, *it happened and it never did*' (p. 35). Throughout this chapter – and throughout the whole novel – a number of stories are referred to. Consider how many you can find in this section, whether they are just legends – like the pot of gold at the end of the rainbow (p. 36) – or specific cultural references – like the *St Trinian's* film (p. 42) or *Little Lord Fauntleroy* (p. 45). Jot down these stories as you come to them. If you don't know what they allude to, look them up. Then consider

how the cumulative effect of all these allusions works. What images do they evoke? Comment on the ways in which they make a particular texture and richness in the novel.

Focus on: visible but unseen

INTERPRET . . .
— Read the passage on p. 42 from 'January, 1961' to 'only the jug on his head'. Think carefully about the account of the person who had to carry a pitcher full of water through a holiday crowd without spilling a drop. Interpret the meaning of the story. Relate it to Saladin's experience of London.
— Then look at the interview with Rushdie and the passages where he speaks about the things that are 'visible but unseen' (pp. 31–2). Relate his account of people's 'blindness' to this story in the novel.

MAKE UP YOUR OWN . . .
— Consider the story of the water carrier again. Then look at the story of Saladin eating the kipper, bones and all, on p. 44. Think about how these stories are parables designed to tell you something about the world and our place in the world; designed also to make you think and to make you come to some moral or philosophical conclusion.
— Then think of an important philosophical or moral point that you would like to make, and illustrate it by making up a story along these lines. If you need more inspiration, read some of Jesus's parables in the New Testament. The story of the prodigal son, for instance, or the parable of the talents, or the story of the good shepherd.

PART I, CHAPTER 3
SECTIONS 6–8 (pp. 46–51)

Focus on: the theme of father and son

DESCRIBE . . .
— Give an account of the relation between Saladin and his father based on this passage. Consider how this might relate to the stories you have already heard about Gibreel and his father.
— If you look ahead to the end of the novel you will see that it concludes with Saladin's reconciliation with his father at his father's deathbed. In the interview, Rushdie speaks on p. 28 about this ending and how he came to write on the theme of reconciliation and forgiveness between father and son.

PART I, CHAPTER 3
SECTIONS 9–17 (pp. 51–73)

Focus on: nationality and difference

TRACE . . .
— Zeeny challenges Saladin's concept of his own national identity. Work through all her complaints about how un-Indian he has become. How does this section – and her characterisation – help to raise questions about identity, nationality, origin and difference?

Focus on: the theme of father and son

TRANSFORM TO WRITE OUT A NEW SPEECH . . .
— In Section 14 of this chapter (p. 69) from 'Of what did the son accuse the father?' to 'a magic lamp', we have a third-person account of what Saladin said to his father. Retell the

story by writing it out in the first and second person as if Saladin were speaking as 'I' directly to his father as 'you'. What does he say? What words does he use? What phrases and images? Stick as closely as you can to the words and phrases used in the original Rushdie paragraph. When you have done this, ask yourself if this exercise has in any way changed your attitude to Saladin or to his father.

ADJUDICATE . . .

— On p. 71 Zeeny is asked to judge between Saladin and his father. You do the same. Whose side are you on? Why? When Zeeny makes her decision what do you think of it?

PART I, CHAPTER 4
(pp. 74–87)

Focus on: heroism

ASK YOURSELF . . .

— Is Tavleen a hero? What is heroism? Do any of the passengers on the hijacked aircraft behave heroically?

Focus on: names

LOOK BACK . . .

On p. 83 Saladin's abbreviated name of 'Chamcha' is discussed. Look back at the passage where his name was first discussed and consider the applications of its meaning here.

Looking over Part I

QUESTIONS FOR DISCUSSION OR ESSAYS

1. 'Some migrants are happy to depart' (p. 19). Discuss, in relation to the themes of Part I.

2.   'If you live in the twentieth century you do not find it hard to see yourself in those, more desperate than yourself, who seek to shape it to their will' (p. 79). Discuss the ways in which 'desperate' characters in this section of the novel seek to shape the world to their will.

3.   Compare and contrast the characters of Gibreel and Saladin as you understand them so far.

4.   Describe the ways in which the theme of relations between father and son has been set out in Part I.

5.   Consider the importance of EITHER Rekha Merchant, OR Alleluia Cone, OR Zeenat Vakil at this point in the novel.

6.   In the interview on pp. 25–6 Rushdie compares his method of writing with the (apparently) haphazard arrangements of jazz. How would you explain his use of that technique in relation to Part I?

PART II: MAHOUND

CHAPTER I
(pp. 91–126)

Focus on: the theme of devils and angels

ANALYSE . . .
— List the different ways in which the idea of the angelic and the devilish is used in this opening section and consider how it relates to the themes of angel versus devil in the novel so far.

Focus on: the idea of the fabled city

COMPARE . . .

— The description of Jahilia is strange and magical, as the bizarre and the real and the imaginary jostle together. Consider the idea of the fabled city, hidden away, lost to time or concealing secret worlds. You might like to look up the story of the lost city of Atlantis. Or else consider how many stories you can think of that work around ideas to do with great cities submerged by water or buried in sand. Any such legend or fairy story will do. You might also like to look at Italo Calvino's *Invisible Cities* (1972) or else to seek out Jeanette Winterson's short story 'Turn of the World' in *The World and Other Places* (1996). Why do you suppose that the idea of a sophisticated and lost city of this kind is so appealing? Why do you imagine that Venice, crumbling into the sea, has such a hold on the Western imagination? In what ways does Rushdie's evocation of Jahilia work on these preoccupations?

Focus on: the idea of poetry and the title

MAKE CONNECTIONS . . .

— On p. 101 Baal is commissioned by Abu Simbel to write some verses. Later on, on p. 114, Mahound recites some verses in the poetry tent. Later still, on p. 124, the verses are mentioned again and specific reference is made to 'the repudiation of the Satanic verses'. How does this section about poetry and prophecy and power relate to the themes of the novel as a whole?

RESEARCH AND COMPARE . . .

At the end of the novel Rushdie notes that the quotations in his text that come from the Quran are taken from two English translations, one by N. J. Dawood and one by Maulana Muhammad Ali. If you can find either of these two translations, look them up and compare the versions of words from the Quran that appear in this section.

Focus on: narrative and narrator

IS THIS A JOKE? . . .

— 'The water-carrier Khalid is there, and some sort of bum from Persia by the outlandish name of Salman, and to complete the trinity of scum there is the slave Bihal' (p. 101). Is this a joke? The water-carrier, the foreign 'bum' and the slave are the outcasts, but their function as a centre for moral authority will become important. Look out for any more references to 'Salman', and keep assessing how this character functions as a teasing representative of the narrator (or even of the author . . .). To begin with, look ahead to p. 105 and check out Salman's role and voice in the events that take place there.

Focus on: mythological beasts

RESEARCH . . .

— On p. 115 the 'manticore' is described. If you look at the Acknowledgements, you will see that Salman Rushdie says that his description of this beast comes from Jorge Luis Borges's *Book of Imaginary Beings*. On p. 117 you will find a list of other mythological beasts or composite beings, part animal, part human. Research all these beasts or mythological creatures and find out what they are supposed to look like and what their special qualities or attributes are supposed to be.

— Why do you suppose so many strange creatures have been imagined? What do they represent or supply in the human imagination?

— How many other such beasts and creatures can you list? Draw them from any source. You might look at the story of Grendel's mother in the Old English poem *Beowulf*. Or you might read J. R. R. Tolkein's *Lord of the Rings* (1954–5) or J. K. Rowling's *Harry Potter and the Philosopher's Stone* (1997).

MAKE UP . . .
— Invent a new mythological beast and write out its description in 500 words. Then consider where you have got its various parts from. How far does each of those parts have a purely physical function and how far might you have invested each of those parts with a more imaginatively or morally significant importance?

ASK YOURSELF . . .
— Is there any way in which you can make a literary analogy or comparison between the styles of writing and the scenes and events that make up *The Satanic Verses* and the idea of the composite mythological beast?

Focus on: allusion

CONSIDER . . .
— On p. 118 reference is made to 'A prophet, Isa, born to a women named Maryam, born of no man under a palm-tree in the desert.' Who is this?

Looking over Part II

QUESTIONS FOR DISCUSSION OR ESSAYS
1. 'Question: What is the opposite of faith? Not disbelief. Too final, certain, closed. Itself a kind of belief. Doubt' (p. 92). Discuss, in relation to Part II.

2. Consider the idea of the fabled city as portrayed in Part II.

3. 'Journeying itself was a home' (p. 94). How is this idea worked out in the novel so far?

4. 'Here's a great lie ... the pen is mightier than the sword' (p. 102). Weigh up this statement in the light of the events of the novel so far.

5. Assess the attitudes to poetry set out in Part II.

PART III: ELLOWEN DEEOWEN

CHAPTER I
(pp. 129–42)

Focus on: hauntings

LIST AND ASSESS ...
— Note down all the references to ghosts and hauntings that you can find in this chapter. Remember to include other words like 'revenant'. How many 'ghosts' can you think of that we have encountered in the novel so far? What does the prevalence of ghosts suggest about the novel's scope in terms of time and space, and in terms of the physical and the spiritual?

CONNECT TO OTHER EVENTS ...
— Thinking about the idea of the fall, connect the images that you collected earlier to other situations. For instance: during the commemorations held on 11 September 2002, to mark the first anniversary of the terrorist attacks on the World Trade Center in New York, 3,000 rose petals were dropped from the gallery of St Paul's Cathedral in London over the congregation gathered there to take part in a service of remembrance. It was 3,000 to symbolise the number of the dead, but the special poignancy of that artistically realised memorial moment was to do with the notion of 'falling'. Think again about these terms and phrases and the episodes in history to

which they relate: 'the Fall'; 'a fall'; 'a falling off'; 'to fall'; 'a dying fall'; 'a fallen woman'; 'the fallen'. You might also consider the literary and poetic implications of the fact that – in the United States and in Canada – the season of autumn is called 'the fall'.

ASSESS AND RELATE . . .
— The narrator refers to 'Higher Powers' and then says '(I am, of course, speaking of myself)' (p. 133). If the narrator is a 'Higher Power' and he is pontificating on the metaphoric significance of the fall, then what might this suggest about the character of the narrator's role, or the author's role? To whom is he – slightly teasingly – comparing himself?

Focus on: satire

COLLECT AND NOTE . . .
— Look at the descriptions of the three police officers who come to investigate the allegations about a possible illegal immigrant. You will find this on p. 139. One of the officers is described as emitting a 'hiss'; another is described 'moaning'; the third – we are told – 'rolls his eyes'. Now look at p. 141 where this triumvirate is labelled 'Hisser Moaner Popeye'. What do you make of this? How have they been turned into stereotypes? And how have their individual (?) actions been turned into stereotypical activities?
— Remember this and think about it in relation to the scenes that follow.

PART III, CHAPTER 2
(pp. 143–56)

Focus on: fairy tales and sorceresses

RESEARCH AND COMPARE . . .

— This chapter begins with a formula that is a favourite with Rushdie: 'It was so, it was not, in a time long forgot . . .' (p. 143). It is a fairy-tale beginning. Look through this chapter and find as many examples of fairy-tale language as you can. Write them down. Write down also the source of your memory that connects to the Rushdie.

— Then look particularly at the people who tell the fairy stories. How often are they portrayed as storytellers in their own right? Enchantresses who hold the listener under their spell? Look up Scheherazade. Look up Circe. Look up the story of the Sirens, Morgan Le Fay and the story of Mother Goose.

— What does this tell you about a) concepts of femininity, b) storytelling, c) repetition, and d) magic and ritual?

PART III, CHAPTER 3
(pp. 157–71)

Focus on: satire

WHAT DOES IT SUGGEST? . . .

— The three police officers who became collectively 'Hisser Moaner Popeye' are now given their real names – Stein, Novak and Bruno. What does this suggest about their origins? Why is this a satirical portrait of the role of the immigration officer in Britain?

Focus on: Englishness

COLLECT . . .

— Look through this chapter and note down each instance where something quintessentially English is mentioned: Kipling on p. 158, for instance, or the Queen on p. 169. When you have completed your list consider how real or how stereotyped this collective image of England and Englishness might be. In the light of the events that are happening to Saladin at this point, how ironic is this image?

Focus on: metamorphosis

RESEARCH . . .

— Saladin turns into a beast, half man and half horned goat in this chapter. Firstly, look up the meaning and derivation of the word 'metamorphosis'. Then find out whatever you can about other such literary metamorphoses whether in legend or fairy tale. You might like to read an English translation of the series of stories by the Roman writer Ovid called *Metamorphoses*. How does Rushdie treat the subject of metamorphosis? You might like to look at Rushdie's essay on the writer Christopher Ransmayr, in *Imaginary Homelands: Essays and Criticism 1981–1991* (1992).

PART III, CHAPTER 4
(pp. 172–88)

Focus on: voices

DISCRIMINATE AND ASSESS . . .

We are told a great deal about Pamela's voice in this chapter and the ways in which her hearty upper-class accent had influenced the attitudes that other people had towards her and the assumptions they made. Remember also that Saladin is all voice – he can turn his voice to mimicking anyone and anything. So he is hidden and yet his voice is heard everywhere.

— Pick out all the relevant passages about voices in this chapter. Then – using that material – think about the importance of voices, of being able to speak, and consider the ways in which people react to others' accents or dialects or ways of speaking.

RESEARCH AND LIST . . .

— How many phrases can you think of which use the idea of voices? What does it mean to 'have a voice', to 'be struck dumb', to 'lose your voice', to have 'the cat get your tongue', to 'hear voices'? If a person in a story is dumb, what does that suggest about their role and place and influence in the world? Examples might include the Little Mermaid who has to lose her voice in Hans Christian Andersen's story, or Philomela, or Lavinia in Shakespeare's *Titus Andronicus*. If you don't know any of these stories look them up.

PART III, CHAPTER 5
(pp. 189–202)

Focus on: hauntings

CONSIDER . . .

— How many new ghosts and hauntings are added to the collection in this chapter? What do they add to the theme of 'the visible but unseen', and the theme of the mingling of the physical and spiritual worlds?

Focus on: colour

ASSESS . . .
— How does this section develop the association of white-ness with the character of Alleluia Cone?

Focus on: feet

THINK ABOUT . . .
— Read the passage on p. 197 about Allie and her bad feet and consider the reference to the fairy story of the sea woman who exchanged her fins or her tail for feet but had to suffer the sensation of knives plunged into her feet at every step. (This is the story of the Little Mermaid also.)
— Then think about feet and different cultural attitudes to feet. What did it mean when Jesus undertook to wash the dis-ciples' feet? Look up the story in John 13 if you don't know it. Or else consider the ancient Chinese practice of footbinding for aristocratic women. Find out what it actually meant and why it was done. Or else read the story of *The Red Shoes* by Hans Christian Andersen – what does that suggest about com-pulsion and social pressures?
— When you have collected a few such stories, make a list – not of the facts of these examples, but of their metaphoric social and cultural meanings. With that list of meanings, think again about the fact that Allie has fallen arches and difficulty in walking as a result. What – in terms of metaphor – might that suggest about her?

Looking over Part III

QUESTIONS FOR DISCUSSION OR ESSAYS
1. 'We can hurt each other with memories two decades old' (p. 179). Discuss, in relation to the book as a whole.

2. Consider the ways in which the narrative of *The Satanic Verses* uses different characters' different points of view.

PART IV: AYESHA

CHAPTER I
(pp. 205–40)

Focus on: dreams

CONNECT . . .
— How many dreams have we heard in the novel so far? What is the importance of dreams and dreaming in *The Satanic Verses*? How do they contribute to the tone of the novel overall?

Focus on: metamorphosis and transformation

RESEARCH AND LOOK BACK . . .
— Look up the meaning of 'butterfly' in a dictionary of symbols. What does the butterfly symbolise and why? Look back at the section where you investigated metamorphosis in Part III. What kinds of metamorphosis happen in this chapter and how do they connect to the image of the butterfly? Consider particularly the story of Ayesha's union with an angel on pp. 225–6. Look up any story you can find that tells of a mortal woman who becomes the lover of a god: the stories of Danae, Europa, Leda, Psyche or Persephone might be good places to start. Look them up in a dictionary of classical mythology. What metamorphoses and transformations happen in those stories? What generally happens to the women in the end? How do those stories of transformation relate to the story of Ayesha? In what ways does her transformed self begin to transform others?

Looking over Part IV

QUESTIONS FOR DISCUSSION OR ESSAYS

1. 'The mystical experience is a subjective, not an objective truth' (p. 239). Discuss in relation to this section and to the novel as a whole.

2. Consider the theme of transformation in the novel so far.

3. In what ways does the portrait of Ayesha compare with that of Pamela, or Zeenat, or Rehka Merchant, or Alleluia Cone?

4. 'Everything is required and everything will be given.' How might you make this a maxim for the experience of the reader of *The Satanic Verses*?

PART V: A CITY VISIBLE BUT UNSEEN

CHAPTER I
SECTIONS 1–3 (pp. 243–53)

Focus on: language

ANALYSE AND INTERPRET . . .

— Look at the opening page of this chapter (p. 243). How many paragraphs and sentences make up this opening page? Now focus on each sentence individually. Work your way through the second sentence teasing out its different clauses. How do you understand it? How many sentences would you divide it into?

— When you have worked your way through subdividing the section and teasing out individual clauses, interrogate the language to answer the following questions:

- Why do think Rushdie opens the section with italics? How does this highlight or privilege the sense of this section?
- What themes are established in the second sentence? Do they support the thematic concerns of the opening sentence?
- Look at the use of quotation marks. Who is speaking? Who is being spoken to? Is the reader being spoken to directly?
- Do you find the language difficult? How many words (if any) are unfamiliar to you? Did you look them up?
- Extend this analysis of your attitude towards the language to consider how this language highlights the themes you have identified.

EXTEND . . .

— 'Her language: obliged, now, to emit these alien sounds that made her tongue feel tired' (p. 249). Having examined these linguistic and thematic concerns, extend your analysis to the section as a whole and think about language. You may want to reapply the questions suggested above. Are the themes you identified in this opening page reflected in the section as a whole?

— Do the sentences remain as long and complex? If the sentences become shorter consider Rushdie's reasons for opening the section in this way. Think overall about this section's treatment of language, both as a theme, and in his deliberate use of a linguistically complex style.

PART V, CHAPTER I
SECTIONS 4–6 (pp. 253–64)

Focus on: the theme of Heaven and Hell

DISCOVER AND PONDER . . .

— 'Do Devils suffer in Hell? Aren't they the ones with the pitchforks?' (p. 254). Look at the treatment of Heaven and Hell in this section. How does Rushdie reference them, playing on commonly held myths about both 'locations'? For example, 'You needn't look so fish-faced and holy' (p. 264). Why include a reference to fish here? How are they associated with things 'holy'?

— When you come across words or phrases you are not sure of, discover what they refer to by either asking someone or using reference texts. How does your understanding of 'Shaitan' (p. 257) influence your attitude to this section?

— When you have picked out and discovered specific references within the text, draw up a list of the terms you associate with Heaven and Hell, such as truth, angels and whiteness as opposed to darkness, devils and criminality. Take some time to extend your list, making it as comprehensive as you can.

DISCUSS . . .

— Get together, in groups, and compare the list you have constructed about the oppositions between Heaven and Hell. Which terms to you regard as the antithesis of one another? Which choices surprise you? Which associations spring up again and again?

— Talk about the common conceptions linking your different versions of these concepts. What influences do you notice informing your definitions, for example religious commitment, age, gender?

LINK . . .

— When you have discussed your differing versions, come to a collective definition, and highlight the particular oppositions you regard as central to constructions of Heaven and Hell.

— Now turn your attention back to the text itself and consider how the oppositions you have identified feature in this section. For example, how is criminality introduced in this section? Who is perceived to be 'guilty' of a crime here? Who is regarded as 'devilish'? How do ideas about darkness and lightness impact upon this section?

— Come back to your working definition as you work your way throughout the text. Think about how these oppositions are complicated at various points. You may want to pick one particular opposition and trace its development, such as the relationship between goodness and whiteness as Rushdie complicates it.

PART V, CHAPTER I
SECTIONS 7–8 (pp. 264–74)

Focus on: the theme of 'Uncle Tom'

IDENTIFY AND ESTABLISH . . .

— This section of the narrative focuses on Chamcha's trip to India and a renegotiation of his identity. He perceives himself to be different from the people he is spending time with, and we are told that even in England he has a particular title: 'When *The Aliens Show* started coming in for stick from black radicals, they gave Chamcha a nickname. On account of his private-school education and closeness to the hated Valance, he was known as "Brown Uncle Tom"' [p. 267]. Uncle Tom is the hero of Harriet Beecher Stowe's novel *Uncle Tom's Cabin*. You may want to read the novel itself, but 'Uncle Tom' has become a frequently used image. Establish (either alone or in groups) what he represents. What is he a short-hand reference for and how is he employed in this context?

CHOOSE AND CONCEPTUALISE . . .
— Look over the passage as a whole and pick out the other figures referred to in this section, paying particular attention to references you recognise as political. For example, how is Margaret Thatcher incorporated here?
— Think about the political framework that is being established here. Work with your teacher, or group leader, to form an understanding of Rushdie's employment of debates about colonisation. Why does he refer to the Falklands at this point? How do the particular references highlighted here work together to produce a political context? (You may want to link this debate to other sections, such as sections focusing on identity politics or colour. Also use the resources provided in the Context section and the Bibliography to help you develop your understanding of the politics you are asked to consider here.)

PART V, CHAPTER I
SECTIONS 9–14 (pp. 275–87)

Focus on: the theme of change

DETAIL . . .
— 'Whether the slowly transmogrifying Saladin Chamcha was turning into some sort of science-fiction or horror-video *Mutey*, some random mutation' (p. 282). Pick out the different references to change in this section:

● List the different words used to describe it (for example, what does transmogrifying mean?).

- Detail the different relationships which are changing here – how are Mishal's relationships with her mother and sister developing?
- What physical changes are catalogued in this section, to both Mishal and Saladin?

EXPLORE . . .

— Develop your analysis of these different elements of change in the section to think about it thematically. How is change presented as a theme here? What parallels do you notice between Mishal and Saladin in their different reactions to change? What explanations are offered for the changes the reader is presented with? Do you accept them as a reader? For example, do the references to witchcraft amuse you or do you take them seriously as an explanation?

EXTEND . . .

— You might like to return to the discussion of change when you think about ideas about religion – for example, fantastic, inexplicable changes are 'miracles'. You could compare the treatment of the 'miracle' with which the novel opens, with the treatment of change here.

PART V, CHAPTER I
SECTIONS 15–19 (pp. 287–94)

Focus on: the theme of anger/hatred

EXAMINE . . .

— 'Another old lady get slice las' night' (p. 287). Examine the treatment of anger and hatred here. Pick out the examples of it in this section. Which characters epitomise these characteristics for you as a reader?

CONSIDER . . .

— When you have teased out the examples of anger you are given here think about Rushdie's reasons for opening this section with references to the 'Granny Ripper' (p. 287). What purpose does this character serve within the text? Why does Rushdie introduce a serial killer? As you work your way through the text, return to the notes you have made and extend them – how do your ideas about this character's function change as you analyse the text as a whole?

INTERROGATE . . .

— Thinking both about the serial killer and about Saladin, interrogate the explanations you are given for the anger the characters discuss. How does Saladin, for example, rationalise his fury? Who does he regard as being responsible for producing this anger in him? Also look at what the anger produces – is anger presented as a positive emotion in relation to Saladin? If so, *how* is it positive?

PART V, CHAPTER 2
SECTIONS 1–3 (pp. 295–308)

Focus on: Alleluia Cone

CHARACTERISE . . .

— These sections trace the history of Alleluia Cone. Work through them, picking out the elements you regard as crucial to an understanding of her and form a character analysis of her. What motivates her? What is she scared of? How is her relationship to her parents offered as an explanation of her character?

— When you have worked your way through these sections

of text and made notes on your understanding of Alleluia, choose ten words that you regard as epitomising her.

DEBATE . . .

— When you have constructed your list, get together as a group and discuss your different choices. Work to construct a collective definition, and argue to support your choices. Why is it important to understand her in the particular terms you have chosen? What textual evidence justifies your choices?

— When you have settled upon a set of terms, you might want to think about her relationship to the other main characters. How do your choices suggest her function within the novel?

PART V, CHAPTER 2
SECTIONS 4–5 (pp. 308–19)

Focus on: knowledge versus belief

EVALUATE . . .

— 'After the news of his death in the plane crash reached her, she had tormented herself by inventing him' (p. 313). Look at Alleluia's changing attitude to Gibreel. How does her affection for him change when she *knows* him to be alive having *believed* him to be dead? Think about the differences between knowledge and belief. How does Rushdie differentiate between the two through tracing Ms Cone's history?

EXTEND AND PONDER . . .

— When you have thought about her change in attitude to Gibreel, extend your analysis to include the treatment of jealousy in this section. Does Gibreel *believe* Alleluia is unfaithful, or does he *know* it? Talk through the complicated understanding of knowledge presented here. Come back to this question as

Gibreel's jealousy resurfaces throughout the novel. You may also want to think about the relationship of belief to religion as referred to in other sections.

PART V, CHAPTER 2
SECTIONS 6–9 (pp. 320–31)

Focus on: the city

DISTINGUISH . . .

— 'London had grown unstable once again' (p. 320). Examine the novel's treatment of London here – how does it form a context for Gibreel? Which landmarks are referred to (p. 327) and how and why does Rushdie distort them?

MAP . . .

— As a group or class look at maps of London. Look at both an *A–Z of London* and an Underground map. You might want to trace some of Gibreel's journeys by looking for the Underground stations he refers to, and finding out where 'Wren's dome' (p. 327) is. Gibreel's narrative is disorientated and confused – discuss why Rushdie sets his decline so specifically.

Focus on: couples

EVALUATE . . .

— Look at the two couples Rushdie parallels here, Rekha and Gibreel, with Orphia and Uriah. Pick out the dialogues they have, or the descriptions of the relationships. What particular information are you given about them?

COMPARE AND CONTRAST . . .

— When you have read carefully through this section focusing on the couples, compare and contrast their relationships. In what ways is Orphia's disappointment paralleling Rekha's? Why do you think Rushdie chooses to establish this parallel? How does Rekha's apparent control of this situation alter your attitude to both couples?

PART V, CHAPTER 2
SECTIONS 10–14 (pp. 331–41)

Focus on: the theme of love

CHARACTERISE . . .

— 'Ah, the power of love' (p. 338). Examine Rushdie's treatment of 'love' in these sections by establishing different characters' understanding of it. For example, how does Rekha's bargaining for Gibreel's affection contrast with Alicja's perception of her daughter's love for Gibreel?

INTERPRET AND COMPLICATE . . .

— When you have analysed the different conceptions of love you are presented with in these sections, consider the novel's treatment of the theme of 'love' here. You might want to introduce other characters or different parts of the text to complicate your analysis. For example, you could contrast Gibreel's relationship with these women with that of Rosa Diamond.

PART V, CHAPTER 2
SECTIONS 15–18 (pp. 341–9)

Focus on: tone and style

DESCRIBE . . .

— 'By the time the Maudsley people felt able to recommend a major reduction in Gibreel's dosages, Sisodia had become so much a fixture [. . .] that when he sprung his trap Gibreel and Allie were completely taken by surprise' (p. 343). Look closely at the tone and style of these sections. What phrases or styles are highlighted for you as a reader? Pick out the literary devices that separate the reader from the community of characters, such as the one indicated above.

CONSIDER . . .

— When you have chosen particular examples, think about Rushdie's reasons for employing such devices. For example, why do you think he gives Sisodia a stutter? How does it affect the reader's attitude to the character and how does it interrupt your reading? How does it establish the narrator as a character? How much do we, as readers, know about him/her? (You could bring in evidence from other sections of the novel.)

DISCUSS . . .

— When you have worked through these devices talk over your responses to them. Think collectively about the *style* of this section, and how it alters your attitude to characters, the plot and the themes you have identified here. For example, how does the narrator's warning that there has been a 'trap' alter your attitude to Sisodia? What does it encourage you to look for while reading?

PART V, CHAPTER 2
SECTIONS 19–23 (pp. 349–56)

Focus on: the theme of insanity

INVESTIGATE . . .

— Gibreel gives an intricate account of the 'strange feeling' (p. 351) that overpowers him as he becomes less rational. Read carefully through these sections picking out the phrases that suggest his illness. How does Rushdie characterise, or describe, Gibreel's 'insanity'?

PARALLEL . . .

— When you have looked closely at this treatment of Gibreel's illness, compare it to other literary versions of mental breakdown. Possibly the most famous contemporary accounts of this experience are Sylvia Plath's *The Bell Jar* and J. D. Salinger's *The Catcher in the Rye*, but you could also look at Robert Louis Stevenson's *The Strange Case of Dr Jekyll and Mr Hyde* (reworked recently in Chuck Palahniuk's *Fight Club*). How do these narratives parallel Rushdie's? In what ways do the protagonists' illnesses mirror one another? What crucial differences do you note?

LINK . . .

— When you have looked at other literary treatments of insanity, focus your attention back on the novel and combine your analyses to consider how differently we read novels that focus upon an apparently mentally ill protagonist. How is our reading altered when we 'discover' the illness? (Here you may particularly want to look at the 1999 film of *Fight Club*.)

Looking over Part V

QUESTIONS FOR DISCUSSION OR ESSAYS

1. Consider the ways in which any ONE of these antitheses is used in this section: black and white, heaven and hell, angels and devils, good and evil.

2. Examine the representation of the equation between goodness and whiteness in this section.

3. Analyse the languages of Part V.

4. Discuss the theme of transformation in *The Satanic Verses*.

5. Explain the importance of the idea of the city in *The Satanic Verses*.

6. Comment on the treatment of madness in Part V.

PART VI: RETURN TO JAHILIA

CHAPTER I
SECTION I (pp. 359–68)

Focus on: the theme of poetry

DEFINE . . .
— 'When Baal the poet' (p. 359) is the opening phrase of this section. Think closely about this clause. Why does the narrator inform us that Baal is a 'poet'? Before going on to consider the narrative's relationship to poetry, spend some time in pairs or threes defining a 'poet' – and what qualifies as 'poetry'. For example, if lines rhyme, are they to be considered

poetry? What, if any, is the difference between song lyrics and poetry?

EXPLORE AND EXTEND . . .

— When you have constructed your version of a 'poet', analyse the section, and you may want to extend this exercise to the whole of Part VI, thinking about the importance of the role of the 'poet' in the story both in terms of plot and theme. Think about the following questions:

- How do our expectations of a 'poet', as opposed to a fireman, inform our expectations for this sub-plot? Are they met?
- In what ways does the narrator play upon our expectations and the poet's ability to manipulate words and meanings?

Focus on: dream versus reality

CONSTRUCT . . .

— 'And Gibreel dreamed this:' (p. 363). This clause appears at significant points in the narrative. Pick out these phrases and consider why they are placed throughout the novel. Think about why the text deliberately highlights that this part of the story is a dream.

FRAME . . .

— When you have considered these references think about how they frame the narrative. What are the major consequences for you as a reader – how are your expectations of plot, for example, changed by the certain knowledge that you are reading a dream?

— Jot down what kind of expectations frame us when we, as readers, encounter a dream narrative. Think about:

147

- Plot
- Characters
- Time – do we expect things to happen in a straightforward order?
- Rules – which do we allow to be broken: physical laws, moral laws?

PART VI, CHAPTER I
SECTIONS 2–6 (pp. 368–80)

Focus on: the theme of blasphemy

EXAMINE . . .

— Using the resources supplied in the text, think and, with the help of your group leader, discover what 'blasphemy' (p. 374) means.

— What kind of vocabulary does 'blasphemy' come from – religious, moral, political?

— Examine the use of words from these vocabularies in these sections, looking closely at the ways they are used. For example, how is 'idol' used (p. 373)?

RELATE . . .

— When you have studied the use of these particular phrases, extend your analysis to consider Baal's actions while in the harem. To what extent do you, as a reader, regard him as blasphemous? Or is it in fact the character of Khalid that the reader perceives to be untrue to his faith?

COMBINE . . .

— If you have undertaken the analysis of 'poetry' and the role of the 'poet' (see previous section), you may want to combine the treatment of blasphemy with the idea of writing, and being original. How much is this battle for truth a battle about words?

PART VI, CHAPTER I
SECTIONS 7–12 (pp. 381–94)

Focus on: heroes

LIST . . .
— Work through the story of Baal's life at the brothel. Pick out the events that make up his time there. Leaving out any qualifying or descriptive terms, draw up a timetable of his actions, culminating in his death.

REVIEW . . .
— When you have completed this, look over your list and consider whether or not, given your list, you would classify Baal as a hero. When you have reached your decision, look back over the text and select evidence to support your view. How do the motivations behind the actions complicate or sustain your argument?

INTERPRET . . .
— Use your analysis of Baal to interpret the idea of the hero. Is a hero someone who performs bold actions? How important is the intention of the hero? Do we expect him to have certain weaknesses or do they detract from his heroism? You may want to think of examples that support your version of the hero.
— When you have formed an idea of what you regard as heroic, consider both Baal and Khalid – to what extent do they meet your criteria?

Looking over Part VI

QUESTIONS FOR DISCUSSION OR ESSAYS

1. Consider the importance of poetry in *The Satanic Verses*, both as a method of narrative and as a theme throughout.

2. Analyse the use and significance of dreams in *The Satanic Verses*.

3. Describe and assess the importance of any ONE or TWO other texts which are alluded to in *The Satanic Verses*.

PART VII: THE ANGEL AZRAEEL

CHAPTER I
SECTIONS 1–2 (pp. 397–408)

Focus on: the theme of love

REVISE . . .
— You may have analysed the different versions of love that Gibreel's lovers have for him (pp. 331–41). If so, look over your notes from that section and remind yourself of your analysis at this point in the text. What particular qualities did you identify as separating Rekha's attitude from Alleluia's, for example? (If you have not attempted the section, you may want to go back or apply some of the tasks to this section of text.)

PARALLEL . . .
'It all boiled down to love' (p. 397). Now look at Saladin's account of love and his relationship to Pamela. This section traces both his conception of love and his understanding that he is no longer in love with Pamela. How does this parallel the

experiences of Gibreel? Look for specific phrases that suggest similarities between the two protagonists here.

CONTRAST . . .

— Look also, however, at the crucial differences between their understandings. How is Saladin clearly set apart from Gibreel in his semi-reconciliation with Pamela?

EVALUATE . . .

— Thinking about these similarities and differences, construct an argument about the novel's treatment of love at this point in the narrative. Would you regard it, for example, as a romantic version of love?

— Select terms to qualify the versions of love you are presented with through the protagonists' relationships.

PART VII, CHAPTER I
SECTIONS 3–10 (pp. 408–19)

Focus on: identity politics

RESEARCH . . .

— 'You don't have to be an angel to be innocent. Unless, of course, you're black [. . .] The point is, this isn't personal, it's political' (p. 412). How do you understand the phrase 'identity politics'? Using the resources you are provided with and with the help of your teacher or group leader, form an understanding of some of the people the text makes reference to, such as Malcolm X (p. 413). Who are they and how do they help you to understand the politics of identity?

CONTEXTUALISE AND RECONSIDER . . .

— When you have researched this term, work together to think about how identity politics are a theme for the novel. Think, for example, about the politics of identity in relation to the identity of the Granny Ripper. (You may want to link it to your analysis of binaries such as heaven and hell, and good and evil.)

PART VII, CHAPTER 2
SECTIONS 1–16 (pp. 420–48)

Focus on: irony

DETERMINE . . .

— Using the glossary provided and your own resources, establish your understanding of the term irony.

DEVELOP . . .

— Examine the sections on pp. 420–31 and 440–8, picking out examples of Rushdie's employment of 'irony' within the text. For example, what is 'ironic' about the setting for this confrontation? How is irony used in the messages Saladin leaves on the couple's answering machine? How is the ultimate assault victim 'ironic'?

Focus on: plot

DESCRIBE . . .

— The setting of the novel changes quite dramatically in the sections on pp. 431–40. Think about the consequences of this for the development of the novel's plot. Read closely through these sections and note the shifts in plot you identify at this point. For example, what do you notice in the developing relationship between Saladin and Alleluia? Link this excerpt back into what happens on either side of it and trace the plot developments of the whole section.

PREDICT . . .

— On the basis of what has occurred and bearing in mind your close reading of the plot of these sections, predict the plot for the rest of the novel. Remember to include characters not mentioned directly but whose roles are central — such as Pamela and Mishal, for example.

EVALUATE . . .

— When you have made your predictions, evaluate what basis you have made them on. How have particular characters as well as the novel's tone and style influenced your decisions? When you have worked through to the end of the novel, look back over your ideas. How do they reflect the novel's development?

PART VII, CHAPTER 3
SECTIONS 1–5 (pp. 449–60)

Focus on: the media

CONTEXTUALISE . . .

— 'Television cameras arrive just in time for the raid on Club Hot Wax' (p. 454). Examine this part of the narrative paying close attention to the role given to the media. How does the presence of television and newspaper journalists form a context for the story's telling? Pay particular attention to the phrases that frame the narrative — in what ways do they suggest media attention?

INTERPRET . . .

— When you have looked at the role the media plays in the narrative, think about the decision to highlight television's reaction to the events that the novel traces. How does the narrator separate a 'media' perception of events from what s/he thinks happened?

INTERROGATE . . .

— Having considered the passage, think about the role of the media as presented by Rushdie here. What sort of a critique is he offering? You could compare this section to his treatment of the film industry at other points in the novel, or you may want to think about contexts for the narrative. Which famous 'media circuses' spring to mind when you think about journalists pursuing people accused of crimes? How does your knowledge of these stories inform your attitude to Rushdie's fictional account?

PART VII, CHAPTER 3
SECTIONS 6–10 (pp. 460–9)

Focus on: the theme of revelation

LIST . . .

— Look through the passage and select the revelations that are made. Remember:

- To think about revelations made to readers AND to characters – what do individual characters learn about one another, for example?
- To look for self-revelations – what do characters learn about themselves?
- To consider revelations that are ONLY made to the reader, but that the characters themselves are oblivious to.

DISCOVER . . .

— When you have constructed a comprehensive list think about the term 'Revelation' itself. It is a book from the New Testament – if you are not familiar with the New Testament, either ask your group leader or investigate its relevance for yourself and come together as a group to understand the term. Use your knowledge to answer the following questions:

- What occurs in Revelation?
- Why is it a relatively famous text?
- What does it predict?

EXTEND . . .

— When you are confident of your understanding, extend your knowledge to the passage as a whole. How does the Book of Revelation inform this passage? How does it play upon associations with it? Also think about how it alters your attitude to the list that you constructed – are the characters undergoing a spiritually fundamental change? How are you left as a reader: what is 'revealed' – in the New Testament sense – to you?

Looking over Part VII

QUESTIONS FOR DISCUSSION OR ESSAYS

1. Consider the presentation of love in Part VII.

2. Analyse EITHER the theme of creation and destruction, OR the theme of revelation in *The Satanic Verses*.

3. Assess the ways in which themes of identity, nationality, race and origins are set out in Part VII.

PART VIII: THE PARTING OF THE ARABIAN SEA

CHAPTER I
SECTIONS 1–4 (pp. 473–82)

Focus on: the theme of pilgrimage

DEFINE . . .

— What is a pilgrimage? Use the various resources you are provided with to discover, and include in your analysis, some famous examples to clarify your understanding. For example, which pilgrimage includes an account of the Parting of the Sea? Make sure your examples are not only Christian. Which faiths, for example, hold pilgrimages to Mecca as a fundamental part of their devotion? Also include secular pilgrimages – people travel from across the globe to celebrate whose birthday at Memphis in Tennessee, USA?

COMPLICATE . . .

— Now turn your attention to the novel and focus on the account of the pilgrimage you are given here. In what ways does it parody the account of pilgrimage that you have developed? Be specific in your analysis and use the examples you have considered in your analysis of the term. How does Rushdie undermine the idea of a sacred journey – look at the specific incidents of the journey, do they parallel other pilgrimages?

PART VIII, CHAPTER I
SECTIONS 5–13 (pp. 482–93)

Focus on: the theme of sacrifice

DETAIL AND DESCRIBE . . .

— In these sections of the novel Ayesha has led her devo-
tees for five weeks. Their pilgrimage enforces a large number
of sacrifices upon the group. Detail those sacrifices and think
closely about how different pilgrims make different kinds of
sacrifices. Describe closely each sacrifice as you perceive it. If
you are in a group you may want to choose specific characters
and pool your reactions so you get really detailed readings.

EXAMINE . . .

— Collate your results and look at the various sacrifices you
have identified. What differentiates them from each other? Do
you regard some sacrifices as being greater than others are? If
so, is your reaction always paralleled by the characters? For
example, when Osman's wife dies, (p. 483) does Ayesha think
it is an enormous sacrifice?

CONSTRUCT . . .

— Think about how the novel's complex version of sacrifice
works in relation to the critique of the pilgrimage you are given
here.

— You may also want to look forward to the rest of this part
of the novel (pp. 494–507) and think about how the outcome
of the pilgrimage affects your reading. Look at the sacrifices
that both the local community and the pilgrims make. Are the
pilgrims vindicated or does the text leave you with an uncer-
tainty that both criticises and supports the pilgrims and their
sacrifices?

PART VIII, CHAPTER I
SECTIONS 14–20 (pp. 494–507)

Focus on: magic realism

DISCOVER . . .

— Magic realism is a literary term; it describes a style used by writers such as Angela Carter and Gabriel García Márquez. Find out what you can about the term. What identifies this group of writers as writing in a magic realist style? What would you expect from the genre?

COMPARE AND CONTRAST . . .

— Look particularly at Gabriel García Márquez's *One Hundred Years of Solitude* (1967), and compare and contrast the two novels as examples of magic realism. For example, *One Hundred Years of Solitude* features a character who is always surrounded by butterflies – in what ways does she parallel Ayesha here?

EXTEND . . .

— When you have looked at the genre as well as specific comparisons between the two novels think about how placing this novel within that genre alters your reading of these sections. If, as a reader, you concentrate upon a style which demands fantastical events and twists in time and space, how does your attitude to the plot and characterisation of these sections of the novel change? (You could extend this to the novel as a whole.)

— You may also want to look back over your reading of the pilgrimage and reconsider your reading of it as a magic realist narrative. Does it change your reading? Do you notice different parts of the story when you consider it as part of this genre?

158

Looking over Part VIII

QUESTIONS FOR DISCUSSION AND ESSAYS

1.   Consider the theme of pilgrimage AND/OR the theme of sacrifice in Part VIII.

2.   Explain Ayesha's role in terms of the novel as a whole.

PART IX: A WONDERFUL LAMP

CHAPTER I
SECTIONS 1–3 (pp: 511–20)

Focus on: titles

INTERPRET . . .
— Before working with the body of the text, think about the title for this part of the novel, 'A Wonderful Lamp'. How do you interpret this title? Does it make sense as it stands? Do you need information from within the novel to understand it? Or does knowledge of a different story help you comprehend the title? Which fairy story does it refer to?

CHOOSE . . .
— Look over the novel as a whole and choose one of the titles given to the nine parts. Now answer the questions raised for 'A Wonderful Lamp' – what do they indicate?

EXPLORE . . .
— Either working through the titles alone, or by allocating them and pooling responses, explore your ideas about the titles. Do they give you the novel's plot? Do they introduce you to specific characters? Do they give you a shortened version of the novel?

REINTERPRET . . .

— Think about how these titles work for you as a reader — you may want to extend your analysis to the novel's title. How do these titles meet or confuse you, the reader? Compare your responses and come back to them when you have completed your analysis.

Focus on: the theme of journeys

CONSIDER . . .

— Look closely at Saladin's account of his journey to see his dying father. Analyse the text's treatment of his journey. How does it mirror an earlier journey? What expectations do we as readers have, given the outcome of his previous flight?

QUESTION . . .

— Use the following questions to interrogate the idea of the journey — you may want to look solely at Saladin's return to India, or you could look at the novel as a whole.

- How does Saladin's physical journey parallel his spiritual one?
- Why is Saladin continuously aware of Gibreel on this journey?
- In which direction is Saladin flying?
- How does this affect our understanding of the journey, as opposed to his initial flight to all things 'English'?

PART IX, CHAPTER I
SECTIONS 4–9 (pp. 520–38)

Focus on: the theme of forgiveness

EVALUATE . . .

— Focus on Saladin's relationship with his father and think about their coming together as a model for forgiveness. How do the two men come to understand choices that previously angered and distressed them? What does Saladin perceive to be different?

— Also think about the role Zeenat plays in the novel's version of forgiveness. How does she enable Saladin to continue after the loss of his father? Think specifically about how she stops Saladin from resuming old battles about property and identity, particularly in relation to the women his father loved.

TALK THROUGH . . .

— Having examined the ways in which characters forgive one another in these sections, talk through the model of forgiveness you are presented with. How do you categorise it? What qualities stand out? Think about the different religious forms of forgiveness and the idea of 'Eastern' and 'Western' morality that Saladin himself explores.

— Again, pay particular attention to Zeenat. (You may want to go back to the beginning and contrast Saladin's relationship with her in his previous encounter with his father to his relationship with her here.)

— Talk about how this novel refuses to give the reader a simple idea of forgiveness. How does Saladin epitomise this complexity?

PART IX, CHAPTER I
SECTIONS 10–15 (pp. 538–47)

Focus on: identity

CHARACTERISE . . .

— The two protagonists are reunited at the novel's climax. Examine the relationship between them closely and produce a character analysis of the two men at the novel's close.

FORMULATE . . .

— Now look at how the two men are opposed – in what ways are they antithetical to one another? Draw up a table which teases out the ways in which they are opposed – for example, Gibreel – Angel, Saladin – Shaitan.

REFLECT . . .

— Examine your list and consider the extent to which the two men are a binary opposition. Do they, in fact, form two halves of one whole? Are they two parts of one individual, and is this why only one of them can survive at the end? Are they two elements which come together to make one story?

Focus on: endings

PONDER . . .

— Analyse this final section of the novel and think about the idea of 'endings'. Saladin says, 'Something is about to happen' (p. 541) – how is expectation constructed for the reader?

COMPARE AND CONSIDER . . .

— When you have thought about how the text builds to its climax, think about how it fits the traditional model of tragedy. The particular tragedy that you might bear in mind here is Shakespeare's *Othello*. Go through Gibreel's final speech on pages 544–5 and see how many points of comparison there may be between the language that Gibreel uses in describing his love for Allie, and the language that Othello uses in describing his love for Desdemona and his jealousy of Cassio. If you read the ending of *The Satanic Verses* as a rewriting of *Othello*, then here 'Iago' survives, or has Saladin developed sufficiently and discarded that identity? (This could be suggested by the subtle change in his name from Saladin to Salahuddin.)

— Is it a happy or a tragic ending?

Looking over the whole novel

QUESTIONS FOR DISCUSSION OR ESSAYS

1. The poet's work – we are told on p. 97 – is 'To name the unnamable, to point at frauds, to take sides, start arguments, shape the world and stop it from going to sleep'. How might this manifesto relate to what Rushdie does in *The Satanic Verses* as a whole?

2. Consider the theme of journeying in the novel as a whole.

3. How are themes to do with colour worked out in the novel as a whole?

4. 'The past is a country from which we have all emigrated' (Rushdie). Discuss, in relation to *The Satanic Verses*.

5. 'Human beings do not perceive things whole; we are not gods but wounded creatures, cracked lenses, capable only of fractured perceptions' (Rushdie). How far is this a prescription for and a description of the method of *The Satanic Verses*?

6. Consider the twin themes of angels and devils in *The Satanic Verses*. Does one dominate, and if not, why not?

7. Does *The Satanic Verses* have a happy ending?

8. What is the role of poetry in *The Satanic Verses*?

Contexts, comparisons and complementary readings

THE SATANIC VERSES

Focus on: history, 'colonial', 'post-colonial' and the interventions of critical theory

RESEARCH . . .

— Lying behind many of Rushdie's books is a sophisticated, knowledgeable, but not uncritical understanding of the history, character, temperament and styles of the Indian subcontinent. In thinking about this area it is absolutely crucial to realise that there are many different kinds of India, and many different shades of 'Indianness'. Not to be aware of this and its implications can lead to a cultural stereotyping which is inappropriate and unhelpful. Rushdie himself makes this point in the essays 'Imaginary Homeland's and 'Outside the Whale', both in *Imaginary Homelands: Essays and Criticism 1981–1991* (1991: Granta and Penguin, London, 1992), pp. 9–21 and 87–101. Read the essays and consider how they relate to *The Satanic Verses* and to the character of his work overall.

— The other thing you can do is to set Rushdie's fictional account of India (or the many Indias) against autobiographical or historical accounts of the events of the twentieth century in India. You could read *The Autobiography of an Unknown Indian* by Nirad C. Chaudhuri (1951), or his later memoir, *Thy Hand Great Anarch!: India 1921–1952* (1987).

— Otherwise, you could take a fiction to compare its portrayal of India with that of Rushdie's. A good choice might be Anita Desai's *In Custody* (1984). Or else try Arundhati Roy's *The God of Small Things* (1997). Rushdie's own short stories, some based on Eastern themes, some on Western themes, might also be helpful; see *East, West* (1995).

— The essential fact of India's variety and multiplicity is further complicated by the ways in which perceptions of the nature of 'history', 'race', 'class' and 'difference' have recently been reinterpreted in the light of critical theory. For a survey of how such themes can be perceived in literature of the past, see, for example, Firdous Azim's *The Colonial Rise of the Novel* (1993) and Gayatri Spivak's essay 'Three Women's Texts and a Critique of Imperialism', in *Critical Enquiry*, Vol. 12, no. 1 (1985), pp. 243–61.

— In order to get a view on how colonial and post-colonial themes have been delineated and applied to more recent works of literature, you might look at Edward Said, *Orientalism* (1978); Gayatri Spivak, *In Other Worlds: Essays in Cultural Politics* (1985); Elleke Boehmer, *Colonial and Post-Colonial Literature: Migrant Metaphors* (1995); Homi K. Bhabha, *The Location of Culture* (1994).

Focus on: tragedy

RESEARCH AND COMPARE . . .

— Look up the strict meaning of tragedy in the glossary of literary terms. Read Shakespeare's *Othello* and consider the ways in which that tragedy can be compared with the 'tragedy' of

The Satanic Verses. In particular, spend some time noting down the ways in which similar metaphors, images and scenes are used in both texts. These areas might include the image of whiteness versus blackness, the exploitation of two settings (Venice and Cyprus in *Othello*, London and various Indian cities in *The Satanic Verses*), the portrayal of murder and suicide, the concept of the celebrity hero and sexual jealousy.

RESEARCH . . .

— To think about concepts of tragedy in general, read Terry Eagleton's *Sweet Violence: The Idea of Tragedy* (2002).

FIND AND READ . . .

— On p. 136 the narrator mentions a story about a man who returns after many years away to discover that his wife has presumed him dead and married another man. He wonders if it was a work by the Victorian poet Tennyson, or by the short-story writer Somerset Maugham. The poem by Tennyson that he is thinking of is called 'Enoch Arden'. Read that poem and consider how the story told there may relate to the themes of *The Satanic Verses*.

— Two other works that use this same plot are the legend of Guy of Warwick and the novel *Sylvia's Lovers* (1863) by Elizabeth Gaskell. Look up either or both of these and compare their themes to those of the Rushdie text.

Focus on: the idea of celebrity

CONSIDER . . .

— If you look at the interview with Rushdie on pp. 30–32 you will see that he discusses the idea of celebrity there and why so many of his works are concerned with the cult of the charismatic personality. Choose any one of the following 'stars'

167

that interests you and find out about them and the ways in which their celebrity cult built up. Then list the key qualities or circumstances of their lives that you think contributed to the way that the public thought and felt about them. When you have done that, look again at the story of Gibreel and consider the ways in which his film-star status may compare with that of your chosen celebrity. Ask yourself why this phenomenon happens and what it might tell you about culture and society in the late twentieth and early twenty-first centuries.

- Elvis
- Marilyn Monroe
- Princess Diana
- John Lennon
- The Kennedys

Focus on: holy books

RESEARCH AND CONSIDER . . .

— Two holy books underpin the references and themes of *The Satanic Verses*. One is the Bible — both the Old and New Testaments — and the other is the Quran. Read the Book of Genesis from The Bible and consider how many elements of the stories told there relate to the stories told in *The Satanic Verses*. Or else read part of the Quran in the English translation by N. J. Dawood and ask yourself the same questions.

Focus on: religious controversy

EXPLORE, COLLECT, INFORM AND ASK YOURSELF . . .

You may know that the publication of *The Satanic Verses* put Rushdie at the centre of a difficult and celebrated row about blasphemy. Many Muslim leaders and thinkers felt that he had overstepped the mark in revising large sections of the Quran and in representing Muhammad, the Prophet of Islam, in an uncomplimentary light. Rallies were held, copies of the book were burned in public and the whole affair came to a climax when Ayatollah Khomeini in Iran issued a *fatwa* on Rushdie, i.e., a sentence of death which implied that any devout Muslim who undertook to kill the author would find his crime sanctioned by the religious leaders and would be promised a reward in heaven. Rushdie had to go into hiding and lived in secret and with heavy police protection for many years. His publishers, both in Britain and elsewhere, were also threatened and one was actually attacked. Recently, the *fatwa* was lifted.

— Collect some information about these events. You may remember the episode, or if not, you might like to ask someone who does remember, what their impressions were at the time. There are also two useful books that you might consult: Malise Ruthven, *A Satanic Affair*, and Lisa Appignanesi and Sara Maitland, eds, *The Rushdie File* (both 1990).

VINTAGE
LIVING
TEXTS

Reference

Selected extracts from reviews

These brief extracts from reviews of Rushdie's work are designed to be used to suggest angles on the text that may be relevant to the themes of the books, their settings, their literary methods, their historical contexts, or to indicate their relevance to issues, questions or problems today.

Sometimes one reviewer's opinion will be entirely contradicted by another's. You might use these passages to ask yourself whether or not you agree with the writer's assessments. Or else you may take phrases from these reviews to use for framing questions – for discussion, or for essays – about the texts.

The excerpts here have been chosen because they offer useful and intelligent observations. In general, though, when you are reading reviews in newspapers, it is best to remember two things: they are often written under pressure; and they have to give the reader some idea of what the book under discussion is like, so they do tend to give space to summarising the plot.

None of these critical opinions are the last word. They are simply contributions to a cultural debate. As such, they should be approached with intellectual interest – because they can give the mood and tone of a particular time – and they should be treated with caution – because the very fact of that prevailing mood and time may intervene.

Victoria Glendinning
From *The Times*, September 1993
On *Midnight's Children*, excess and knowledge

[When Rushdie left Cambridge] he went into advertising. Copy-writing, he has said, taught him to condense.

What *un*condensed Rushdie would be like beggars the imagination. *Midnight's Children* is ambitious, fantastical, satirical, comic, terrifying, a scion of Rushdie's literary 'family' – Cervantes, Sterne, Gogol, Dickens, Grass, Melville, García Márquez, Beckett, Joyce . . . plus American movies, and Hindu epics. Rushdie was displaced geographically and culturally, and by not writing in his mother tongue, which is Urdu. The energy generated by these tensions produced *Midnight's Children*, written about his own country from far away, as Joyce wrote *Ulysses*. In both cases, what came out was a new thing.

'And there are so many stories to tell, too many, such an excess of intertwined lives events miracles places rumours, so dense a commingling of the improbable and the mundane!' That is from the first page of *Midnight's Children*. Saleem Sinai, the narrator, is one of 1,001 children born with magical powers at the precise midnight moment of India's independence. It makes him feel 'heavily embroiled in Fate – at the best of times a dangerous sort of involvement'. Unreliably – because he could scarcely be a more unreliable narrator – he tells his tale 'with the absolute certainty of a prophet'. The India of the novel is as fantastic and extravagant as a dream. But with hindsight, we can see that Rushdie's fiction has

always been prophetic, as if he knew something that
he did not yet know.

Peter Straus
From the *Literary Review*, August 1997
On the significance and influence of
Midnight's Children

With a fantastic colloquial ear and side-splitting use
of language, Rushdie convincingly undermined previous literary depictions of India by E. M. Forster
and Paul Scott, which seemed to set India and
Indians permanently in the Edwardian era. The
blending of fact with fiction, allied to Rushdie's
great verbal gifts and heavenly imagination, make
this book the colossus it is.

The interweaving of myth and history means that
Midnight's Children has often been read as history in
India, but fiction in Britain. It proved to be a land-
mark. It displayed new methods of narration, mixing
in certain magical elements, echoing South American
writers, and offering a Dickensian sense of caricature
and feel for ordinary people. It has encouraged con-
fidence in the Indian novel, and there is now a
plethora of excellent writing in English by Indians ...
Maybe not surprisingly, *Midnight's Children* has been
surrounded by levels of myth and mystery about its
readability which mirror its own nature. The very
first reader of the manuscript patronisingly called the
novel a 'fat ramble round Indian Rushdie's mind',
and it was only when the publisher Tom Maschler
stated, 'This is a work of genius,' that the belief in

the novel shown by its editor Liz Calder was deemed
to be justified.

Henry Louis Gates, Jr
From *The New Yorker*, 1994
On the theme of migrancy

The literature of migrancy may be the literature of
border-crossing, but Rushdie reminds us that borders
crossed aren't merely the kind drawn in dirt. His
restless intelligence is forever challenging the lines
between East and West, the past and the present,
Homo Ludens and *Homo sapiens*, realism and fantasy.
(He has admitted that the techno-phantasmagorias of
J. G. Ballard strike him as much more 'realistic' than
the ostensibly ordinary settings conjured by Anita
Brookner.) If there are cultural traditions that belong
to the East, there is also, he insists, a third tradition,
a tradition of displacement and exile which belongs
to neither. Of course the big themes of migrancy –
cultural heterogeneity, the fragmented and hybrid
nature of identity – are equally the pet themes of
literary postmodernism. And make no mistake: there
isn't an artist more self-conscious than Salman
Rushdie. (His critical essays bristle with references to
such postmodernist pashas as Michel Foucault and
Jean-François Lyotard.) But the literary resources of
migrancy are more than theoretical. It hasn't escaped
the British literary establishment that a lot of what's
most compelling in contemporary fiction has been
written by people with names like David Malouf,
Timothy Mo, V. S. Naipaul, Caryl Phillips, and, yes,
Salman Rushdie – people who have, in one way or

another, dwelled at the margins of the Commonwealth.

'Literature is not in the business of copyrighting certain themes for certain groups,' Rushdie has wisely cautioned. Still, we've all had a chance to see what happens when, as the saying goes, the Empire strikes back.

Robert Coover
From the *New York Times*, 10 January 1995
On literature, history, satire

Mr Rushdie, one suspects, would rather have his work discussed purely as literature, without reference to the unhappy history that has plagued him, but sometimes the stories themselves make it difficult to ignore the story of their author. 'At the Auction of the Ruby Slippers' [from *East, West*], the middle piece of this middle section, and thus the middle of the book as well, is an example. The ruby slippers are of course those worn by Dorothy in *The Wizard of Oz* and, on the surface, the story is a broad socio-political satire, a bit over the top at times, told by a communal 'we' and depicting the current market-based free-for-all as a brutal futuristic hell wherein everything in the world is for sale, with the hoarding of possessions leading to universal paranoia: 'These are uncompromising times,' the narrator says.

Katherine Forestier
From the *South China Morning Post*,
24 September 1994
On the 'fragment' method

Being cut off from his culture has not meant he is
short of ideas. 'You build a story like "The Free
Radio" out of little fragments of things,' he said,
recalling how as a child he used to chat to the rick-
shaw drivers who had a stand near his grandparents'
house.

'If you have enough fragments of a place, enough
angles into a society, you can always find a way of
creating credible fiction. Fiction of course needs a
root in the real world but in the end it has to take
off from that to its own place,' he said.

Stories became stuck together from different
places. 'Short stories spring up almost fully formed
in a way a novel doesn't. A novel requires more
exploration,' he said.

'My processes as a writer just go on irrespective
of what the circumstances in my life might be.' It
was not easy. 'But then writing never is,' he added.

Fay Weldon
From the *Literary Review*, October 1994
On language and style

Good to see the Rushdie genius still there and func-
tioning in the face of all politico-religious/pseudo-
literary attacks upon it – perhaps even improved,
certainly made more accessible to the timorous by
the need for brevity. Shivers-up-the-spine time again:

a kind of exhilarated singing in the ears, at least in mine – what I imagine the music of the spheres to have been – in the cumulative effect of this collection of short stories. Hard to put a defining finger on the secret of Rushdie's particular literary magic, let alone emulate it.

D. J. Taylor
From the *Independent*, 9 October 1994
On language and method

Terse and simply written in the gnomic repartee of the inarticulate, these pieces [*East, West*] have something of the unfeigned, stark quality of the late Shiva Naipaul's early stories, although 'unfeigned' is never a safe adjective to use in connection with Rushdie. The sinister political backdrop to 'The Free Radio', for instance, is cunningly woven into the account of Ramani's day-dreams, and the 'arm-banded cronies' who surround the official caravan with its stink of ether are an ominous incidental presence.

Homi K. Bhabha
From the *Guardian*, 4 October 1994
On themes and methods

For a writer whose fiction spans some of the most contentious fault lines of cultural debate – metropolis/periphery, atavarism/modernity, fundamentalism/multi-culturalism – Salman Rushdie has a fine sense of the little things of life. Everyday events guide his wily narrative gift. In *Midnight's Children*, it is the tic and twitch of Padma's thigh muscles, as they respond to every twist and turn in the story of Cyrus the Great, that provide Saleem Sinai with his first lesson in story-telling: '. . . what happened is less important than what the author can persuade his audience to believe'. And something very similar to such a willing suspension of disbelief is demanded of the reader of *The Satanic Verses*, where the mythic locations of sacred names and places suddenly take on a new and lucid life in the prosaic neighbourhoods of contemporary London or Bombay . . . *East, West* furnishes the little room of literature with a voice that rises from the 'comma' that both divides and joins East and West. At a time when writers and critics are concerned with the 'hyphenated' realities of being Afro-Caribbean, or Asian-American, Rushdie writes from the more fluid perspective of the comma, where histories of cultural difference exist side-by-side, in a state of creative interruption or interpolation.

'But I, too, have ropes around my neck, I have them to this day, pulling me this way and that, East and West, the noose tightening, commanding, choose, choose. I buck, I snort, I whinny, I rear, I kick . . . I refuse to choose.'

It is, of course, only from a position of relative privilege — class, power, education, profession — that one can choose *not to choose*, though in no way does this invalidate the individual, existential predicament dramatised above. There is, in the best of these stories, a coming to terms, in the subtlest way, with what it means to be a post-colonial cosmopolitan. This does not 'buck' the larger histories of colonial

migration or diaspora, as much as it explores that
stage of psychic realignment that Naipaul has beauti-
fully named 'the enigma of arrival'.

John Carey
From the *Sunday Times*, 2 October 1994
On method, style and form

What then does *East, West* suggest about the
progress of the Rushdie experiment? It tells us that
his storytelling powers are alive and well – his inge-
nuity, wit, charm and his restless talent for the un-
expected. One of the several astonishing things
about the book is its compression. The uncanny ear
for argot and idiom . . . can bestow individuality on
a speaker in the space of a few syllables. Equally
dazzling is the book's scope. You are amazed,
looking back, at the different fictional worlds its nine
brief stories have carried you through – much as
travellers on magic carpets must wonder, on landing,
at the frailty of their craft. Nor is this versatility gra-
tuitous. Mixing different story-modes – *Arabian
Nights*, 18th-century English, futurist – has, for
Rushdie, a political meaning. The 'hotch-potch'
effect, as he has called it, is a counter-measure
against ideas of purity – pure race, pure culture,
pure religion – which have proved to be the seed-
beds of atrocity.

Pico Iyer
From the *Times Literary Supplement*,
29 September 1994
On language, the character and placing of his
writing, and head versus heart

This most current and *au fait* of writers has, even in
his most casual mode, a genius for all the old-fashioned skills – language and story-telling and imagination. And the beauties of these pieces come often
from their impenitent gift, and zest, for language:
from the way *rutputty* and *khichri* and *funtoosh!* are
smuggled into standard English; from the delight
Rushdie takes in 'hicksville' and 'spooks' (as a verb),
in the 'hydravarious' sounds of our promiscuous
global village; from his grasp of a sensibility that
none of his London friends could muster ('Two
mouthfuls are better to eat than wind'). The collection is, at times, a glorious Hobson-Jobson of post-
colonial usage, the product of a man who is at home
enough in any culture to bring equal-opportunity and
irreverence to all.

In that sense, these stories really do underline
what has been implicit all along: that Rushdie is the
great post-imperial Indian writer, bringing the sounds
of India into an England that has often sustained a
more quaintly domesticated notion of the subcontinent. Though trained in England – perhaps because
trained in England – Rushdie has greater ease with
India than many Indians who grew up at home
under English tutelage: his is, truly, the voice of an
independent nation (and, therefore, a polyglot pop
culture). His is a world in which Indian boys in
Kensington sing Neil Sedaka songs to baby girls

called Scheherazade; and where diplomats from Asia play out the *Star Trek* fantasies they hatched in Dehra Dun. It is a world where Indians from Cambridge learn about gurus from mad Englishmen, and Jimmy Greaves meets Fred Flintstone, to the tunes of Ravi Shankar. And when, in passing, he notes that 'Home, like Hell, turned out to be other people', it becomes not just a witticism, but a touching cry of need.

Rushdie, in fact, is always strongest when leading with his heart.

Gillian Boughton
From *Third Way*, May 1999
On style and themes

Rather like Lord Byron, Rushdie is a wanderer, a voluntary exile and a causer of outrage. Like Byron, he betrays a preoccupation with the concept of the damnation of angels. Like him, he writes at virtuoso length, delighting in wit and *double entendre* and allusion, both classical and contemporary. And, like him, he has huge appeal.

What is his message? It seems, that every individual life is, in one sense, a microcosm of all lives. This was wonderfully true of *Midnight's Children*, 'the Booker of Bookers' in 1993 . . . 'The world is not cyclical, not eternal or immutable, but endlessly transforms itself, and never goes back, and we can assist in that transformation.' In this respect, his world is not without hope.

Anon
From 'Books that Shaped the Century',
Publishing News, 24 September 1999

Would you recognise this book?

The Satanic Verses, by Salman Rushdie. This book is
an allegorical novel involving the bizarre dreams of
one of two survivors of a terrorist attack on an Air
India plane.

Glossary of literary terms

Absurd A term often used to designate the pointlessness and irrationality of human existence. Samuel Beckett's play *Waiting for Godot* (1952), where two tramps or clowns or displaced persons debate the meaning of life while they wait for someone or something that never appears, is the best-known example.

Allusion Where deliberate mention is made of some other literary text, cultural phenomenon or historical fact.

Analogy One item or example is explained by means of a comparison with another item or example.

Assonance A poetic technique where words are used in sequence for an effect created by the fact that they employ similar sounds. For example, Tennyson's 'immemorial elms'.

Autobiography Where the story of a life of an individual is told by that person himself or herself. 'Auto' means 'self'.

Binary oppositions Binary suggests 'two', so an array of opposites set out in twos. For example: black and white, good and evil, the whore and the Madonna.

Carnivalesque Based on the idea of the 'carnival' where traditionally the world is turned topsy-turvy, so servants are in charge, men and women exchange clothes, identities are swapped. It implies a joyous anarchy.

Comedy A play (or other work of literature) designed to

entertain, and perhaps also to amuse. It will (generally) have some basis in real life; it will also end happily.

Composite figure An image made up of more than one item: For instance, the idea of an 'elephant man' is a composite figure.

Conceit An elaborate or far-fetched image or metaphor designed to help describe a thing. Such a comparison is more ingenious than true. A well-known example is in John Donne's poem 'A Valediction Forbidding Mourning', where the two parting lovers are represented as the two arms of a compass which may go further away from each other as they transcribe the circle, but which are not entirely separated.

Difference In the ordinary sense, being 'other than' the subject or the centre. 'Difference' has come to mean, as strictly literary critical term, where you stand with a 'one' that is a given – e.g., 'man' – then you set up an 'other' that is often conventionally (however rightly, wrongly or appropriately) defined in relation to, and in terms of its 'difference' from, it – e.g., 'woman'.

Direct speech Where the speech of the speaker is represented as it was actually said. ' "Do you want to go now?" he said'. As opposed to indirect speech: 'He asked if I wanted to go.'

Fable A tale that may not be true, or has moved into legend and fame in such a way that it takes on some iconic significance. More strictly, an allegorical story that emphasises a moral theses.

Fairy tale Literally a tale told about or by fairies – 'Les Contes des Fees' in French – but from the eighteenth century on, when many oral stories came to be collected and written down, a story that has many incarnations but is often formulaic, and that will begin with a patterned opening – 'Once upon a time' – and end in some predictable way – 'and they all lived happily ever after'. If such stories do not have a moral content, they very often do have some social agenda.

Fantastic Related to the description of 'fantasy'.

First person 'I', as opposed to 'he'.

Grotesque Concerning the fantastic and extravagant distortion whether of human features or characteristics.

Indirect speech 'He told me that the earth was flat', as opposed to direct speech, '"The earth is flat," he said.'

Intertextuality The name given to the practice of artistically invoked reference to another key text. So, for instance, John Milton's *Paradise Lost* is a work intertextually linked with the Bible.

Irony A subtle method of conveying some counterpoint or inconsistency which may be humorous or sad. Dramatic irony is when the reader – for example – knows more about what is going on than the character and can therefore sadly, or amusedly, predict the clash that will come. Verbal irony is a statement in which what is ostensibly said is different from what is implied.

Legend An hereditory story which lies somewhere between myth and historical fact and which, as a rule, is about a person, not a supernatural being.

Leitmotiv Strictly speaking, a musical term for a phrase of a few bars that will recur and that is specifically associated with a character or a theme. In the overture to Bizet's opera *Carmen* there is a 'fate theme' which is repeated at key moments in the telling of the doomed love affair between the soldier Don Jose and the gypsy Carmen. In literature this might be a phrase or description associated with a particular character or theme and it will recur so that the reader acquires a competence that enables them to recognise the leitmotiv at each return and connect it to that character or theme. Ayesha's butterflies in *The Satanic Verses* are one example. Dickens's setting up Arthur Clennam's perception of Flora Finching as a 'moral mermaid' in his *Little Dorrit* is another.

Lyric The derivation of the word relates it to the 'lyre', a stringed instrument resembling a harp which in the ancient Greek tradition would accompany the singing of poetry. Lyric is a 'sung' form of poetry (or prose) generally dealing with subjects such as love, loss, nature. It is set against 'epic' poetry which takes as its subject war, heroism, the exploits of gods.

Magic realism A much misused term. It grew out of a particular strand in literature developing from the 1960s on, where 'magic' events would occur in settings that were detailed and 'realistic' in the old-fashioned sense of the Victorian realist novel which sets out to pretend that events being described are – in some sense – a history. In fact, all literature is effectively 'magic' in that it is not real, and all literature is effectively 'realistic' in that it comes from the mind of one person and enters the mind of another. An example of this style might be Angela Carter's novel *Nights at the Circus* (1986) which is set in late Victorian London and describes that scene minutely, but where we are to believe simultaneously that the heroine was hatched out of an egg and has wings.

Melodrama Literally, a drama accompanied by music. But as a result of the nineteenth-century fashion for playing dramatic music to go with sensational plays about murder and horror, it has come to mean anything over the top.

Metamorphosis Where something is transformed from one thing to another literally or metaphorically. A butterfly's metamorphosis from grub to butterfly is literal; your drunken husband turning into a pig is metaphorical.

Metaphor Any figure of speech by which one thing is explained or described by relating it to some other thing. It splits into two elements: the 'tenor' which is the primary subject, and the 'vehicle' which is the secondary figurative term applied to it. For instance, in 'the whirligig of time', 'time' is the 'tenor' or the primary subject because the metaphor is designed to tell us something about the nature of time, and the 'whirligig' is the 'vehicle' because it is the image or figure designed to show what time is like – i.e., it brings everything back round again (and might make you end up disorientated and dizzy).

Mimetic Where literature attempts to 'mime' or to imitate something else.

Naturalism Anything that strives for an effect that seems to be 'natural' as opposed to contrived or artificial.

Parable A story with some kind of moral or socially controlling element.

Paradox Where one thing is apparently contradicted by another, but where, in fact, they are both extant. A 'paradox' picture is one that appears to represent one thing when looked at one way, and another thing when looked at from another angle.

Parenthesis An aside, in brackets.

Pun Where a word or a phrase may have two meaning. Often amusing: for example, 'The provision of toilet paper in a rented cottage is the bottom line.'

Realism A literary technique or term meant to indicate some mimetic element where the text masquerades as 'real' (though we always know it's not). In this way we imagine that the town of Middlemarch in George Eliot's novel of that name (1871–2) is a real place in the middle England of the nineteenth century.

Retrospective narration A story that is told after the events relayed have taken place. Literally a story told 'looking back'.

Rhetoric The deliberate exploitation of dramatic and elaborate language designed to persuade.

Riff A jazz term for a digression or musical improvisation that departs from the main theme for a while, only to return to it later.

Satire A way of writing that employs laughter as a weapon to expose the failings and inconsistencies of characters or systems. George Orwell's *1984* (1949) is one such novel, taking as its subject the totalitarian regimes in Russia and Germany in the first half of the twentieth century (and indeed any such regime anywhere).

Surrealism Something over or above the 'real'. So not real at all.

Symbol A thing that stands for another thing.

Third person 'He' as opposed to 'I'.

Tragedy A serious play (or literary work) showing the downfall of some important character or characters. Sometimes the key to these events is a 'tragic flaw' in the character of the protagonist themselves. In the ancient Greek tradition, it is the highest form of dramatic and literary art.

Biographical outline

1947 19 June: (Ahmed) Salman Rushdie born. The son of Anis Ahmed Rushdie and Negin Rushdie.

1954 Attended Cathedral School, Bombay.

1961 Attended Rugby School in England.

1968 Graduated from King's College, Cambridge with MA (hons) in History.

1975 *Grimus* published.

1981 *Midnight's Children* published. Won the Booker Prize for Fiction, the James Tait Black Memorial Prize and the English Speaking Union Literary Award for *Midnight's Children*.

1983 *Shame* published.

1984 Won the Prix du Meilleur Livre Étranger for *Shame*.

1985 Made *The Painter and the Pest*, TV film.

1987 *The Jaguar Smile: A Nicaraguan Journey* published.

1988 Made *The Riddle of Midnight*, TV film. *The Satanic Verses* published. 5 October: *The Satanic Verses* banned by the Indian government. Won the Whitbread Novel Award for *The Satanic Verses*.

1989 Won the German Author of the Year Award for *The Satanic Verses*. 14 February: Ayatollah Ruhollah Khomeini declared a *fatwa* that sentenced Rushdie and all those involved in the publication of *The Satanic Verses* to death.

1990 *Haroun and the Sea of Stories* published. Won the Writer's Guild Award for *Haroun and the Sea of Stories*.

1991 *Imaginary Homelands* published.

1992 Awarded the Arts Council Literature Bursary Award and the Kurt Tucholsky Prize, Sweden. *The Wizard of Oz* published.

1993 Appointed Honorary Professor at MIT. Won the Prix Colette, Switzerland. Won the Booker of Bookers for *Midnight's Children*.

1994 *East, West* published. Won the Austrian State Prize for European Literature.

1995 Made Dist. Fellow in Lit at UEA and Hon. Doctorate at Bard College. *The Moor's Last Sigh* published. Won the Whitbread Novel Award and the British Book Awards Author of the Year Award for *The Moor's Last Sigh*.

1997 *The Vintage Book of Indian Writing* published.

1998 25 September: The Iranian government ended the *fatwa*.

1999 *The Ground Beneath Her Feet* published. The screenplay of *Midnight's Children* published. Made Commandeur de l'Ordre des Arts et des Lettres.

2001 *Fury* published.

2002 *Step Across This Line* published. Won the London International Writers Award.

Select bibliography

WORKS BY SALMAN RUSHDIE

Grimus (Victor Gollancz, London, 1975; Vintage, 1996)

Midnight's Children (Jonathan Cape, London, 1981; Vintage, 1995)

Shame (Jonathan Cape, London, 1983; Vintage, 1995)

The Jaguar Smile: A Nicaraguan Journey (Pan Books, London, 1987; Vintage, 2000)

The Satanic Verses (Penguin Books, London, 1988; Vintage, 1998)

Haroun and the Sea of Stories (Penguin Books/Granta, London, 1990)

Imaginary Homelands (Penguin Books/Granta, London, 1991)

The Wizard of Oz (British Film Institute Publishing, London, 1992)

East, West (Jonathan Cape, London, 1994; Vintage, 1995)

The Moor's Last Sigh (Jonathan Cape, London, 1995; Vintage, 1996)

Edited with Elizabeth West *The Vintage Book of Indian Writing* (Vintage, London, 1997)

The Ground Beneath Her Feet (Jonathan Cape, London, 1999; Vintage, 2000)

The Screenplay of Midnight's Children (Vintage, London, 1999)

Fury (Jonathan Cape, London, 2001; Vintage, 2002)

Step Across This Line (Jonathan Cape, London, 2002)

INTERVIEWS

P. S. Chauhan, *Salman Rushdie Interviews* (Greenwood Press, London, 2001)

The Salon Interview with Salman Rushdie can be accessed at www.salon.com/06/features/interview.html

CRITICAL WORKS

Fawzia Afzal-Khan, *Cultural Imperialism and the Indo-English Novel: Genre and Ideology in R.K. Narayan, Anita Desai, Kamala Markandaya and Salman Rushdie* (University Park, Pennsylvania State University Press. PA, c.1993).

Lisa Appignanesi and Sara Maitland, eds, *The Rushdie File* (Fourth Estate, London, 1989).

Timothy Brennan, *Salman Rushdie and the Third World, Myths of the Nation* (Macmillan, London, 1989).

Keith Booker, *Critical Essays on Salman Rushdie* (G. K. Hall, New York, 1999).

Catherine Cundy, *Salman Rushdie* (Manchester University Press, Manchester, 1997).

M.D. Fletcher, ed., *Reading Rushdie, Perspectives on the fiction of Salman Rushdie* (Rodopi, Amsterdam, 1994).

Michael Gorra, *After Empire, Scott, Naipaul, Rushdie* (University of Chicago Press, Chicago, 1997).

Damien Grant, *Salman Rushdie* (Northcote House, Plymouth, 1999).

Joel Kuortti, *The Salman Rushdie Bibliography, a Bibliography of Salman Rushdie's Work and Criticism* (Peter Lang, New York, 1997).

Alison Lee, *Realism and Power: Post Modern British Fiction* (Routledge, London, 1990).

Leonard W. Levy, *Blasphemy: Verbal Offense Against the Sacred, from Moses to Salman Rushdie* (Knopf, N.Y., 1993).

Uma Parameswaran, *The Perforated Sheet: Essays on Salman Rushdie's Art* (Affiliated East West Press, New Delhi, 1988).

Margareta Petersson, *Unending Metamorphoses: Myth, Satire and*

Religion in Salman Rushdie's Novels (Lund University Press, Chantwell-Bratt, 1996).

Ralph J. Crane, *Inventing India: A History of India in English-Language Fiction* (Macmillan, Basingstoke, 1992).

Malise Ruthven, *A Satanic Affair* (Chatto & Windus, London, 1990). Gives the political and historical background to the *fatwa* issued against Salman Rushdie.

Bibliographies, biography and some comment are available at www.kirjasto.sci.fi/rushdie.html and www.levity.com/corduroy/rushdie.html

The editors

Jonathan Noakes has taught English in secondary schools in Britain and Australia for fifteen years. For six years he ran A-level English studies at Eton College where he is a house-master.

Margaret Reynolds is Reader in English at Queen Mary, University of London, and the presenter of BBC Radio 4's *Adventures in Poetry*. Her publications include *The Sappho Companion* and (with Angela Leighton) *Victorian Women Poets*.

Also available in Vintage

Salman Rushdie

THE GROUND BENEATH HER FEET

**'Quite simply the most absorbing, the most entertaining
book you are likely to read all year'**
Mail on Sunday

'This is a fabulous, glowing, witty and brilliant epic . . . This is the
Ulysses of rock 'n' roll . . . glittering writing – humane and very funny'
Independent

Vina Apsara, a famous and much loved singer with a wild and
irresistible voice, is caught up in a devastating earthquake and never
seen again. This is her story, and that of Ormus Cama, the lover
who finds, loses, seeks and again finds her, over and over throughout
his own extraordinary life in music. Set in the inspiring, vain, fabulous world of rock 'n' roll, this is the story of a love that stretches
across continents, across Vina and Ormus's whole lives, and even
beyond death.

'The first great rock 'n' roll novel in the English language'
Times

'A ground-breaking work . . . Rushdie turns our century of celebrity
and atrocity inside out. He makes you see the world in a new light'
Time Out

'Uniquely exhilarating . . . Salman Rushdie once more proves his
mastery . . . His sheer linguistic energy is a delight'
Sunday Telegraph

VINTAGE

Also available in Vintage

Salman Rushdie

THE MOOR'S LAST SIGH

Winner of the Whitbread Novel of the Year Award

'A triumph . . . affectionate and masterly'
New York Times Book Review

'A wonderful book, gorgeous in colour and texture,
magnificent in scope, wildly funny'
Independent on Sunday

'Salman Rushdie's latest and – so far – greatest novel . . . held me
in its thrall and provided the richest fictional experience of 1995'
Antonia Fraser, Books of the Year, *Sunday Times*

'Rushdie is still our most exhilaratingly inventive prose stylist,
a writer of breathtaking originality'
Shashi Tharoor, *Financial Times*

'Endlessly inventive, witty, digressional and diverting'
Michael Ratcliffe, *Observer*

V

VINTAGE